The Secrets of ANCIENT MAN

Revelations from the Ruins

DON LANDIS
general editor
with *Jackson Hole Bible College*

Photo Credits: T-top, B-bottom, L-left, R-right, C-Center

Shutterstock.com: pg. 3, pg. 5, pg. 8, pg. 10, pg. 12, pg. 14 (B), pg. 16, pg. 17 (B), pg. 20, pg. 25, pg. 27, pg. 31, pg. 44, pg. 47 (L), pg. 49, pg. 50 (R), Pg. 51 (2), pg. 52-53, pg. 56 (L), pg. 57 (T), pg. 58-59 (T), pg. 58 (B), pg. 62 (C), pg. 64-65, pg. 66 (B-4), pg. 67, pg. 69, pg. 73, pg. 79 (T), pg. 80, pg. 81, pg 83 (2), pg. 84 (B), pg 84 (R), pg. 88, pg. 89, pg. 90, pg. 94 (B), pg. 95 (3), pg. 98 (B), pg. 99, pg. 100, pg. 101, pg. 103 (2-B), pg. 105 (2), pg. 107, pg. 109, pg. 111, pg. 112 (2-T), pg. 113 (T-bkg.), pg. 114, pg. 116 (3), pg. 117 (B), pg. 118 (T), pg. 119, pg. 120, pg. 122 (B), pg. 124, pg. 128, pg. 130

istock.com: pgs. 6-7, pg. 11, pg. 14 (T), pg. 50 (L), pg. 52 (L), pg. 54, pg. 63 (3), pg. 66 (T-3), pg. 76, pg. 82, pg. 96, pg. 118 (C), pg. 121 (L),

Superstock.com: pg. 32; pg. 41 (2), pg. 43 (2), pg. 47 (R), pg. 60-61, pg. 68, pg. 71, pg. 74, pg. 77, pg. 79 (B), pg. 106, pg. 117 (T), pg. 122 (T), pg. 123,

NASA: pg. 33 (T),

Ben Iocco "The Battle Over Nephilim": pg. 4

David S. Lewis (flickr.com/photos/dslewis): pg. 33 (B), pg. 34 (T, C, BL), pg. 84 (T),

Xuan Che (flickr.com/photos/rosemania) flickr commons: pg. 56 (R)

Ken Zuk: pg 34 (BR)

Robert Harding Productions: pg. 46,

Science Photo Library: pg. 110 Pasquale Sorrentino / Science Source

Wikimedia Commons: pg. 18, pg 19 (B), pg. 21, pg. 22, pg. 23, pg. 24, pg. 26, pg. 28-29, pg. 28 (B), pg. 30 (B), pg. 33 (2-C); pg. 35 (3), pg. 36 (2), pg 37, pg. 39, pg. 40, pg. 42, pg. 45 (R), pg. 48, pg. 55 (R), pg. 57 (B), pg. 58 (BL), pg. 59, pg. 61, (BR), pg. 70, pg. 75 (3), pg. 78, pg. 85, pg. 87, pg. 91, pg. 92, pg. 93 (6), pg. 94 (T), pg. 97 (T), pg. 98 (2), pg. 104 (2), pg. 108, pg. 112-113 (B), pg. 115, pg. 127,

Images from Wikimedia Commons are used under the CC-BY-SA-3.0 license or the GNU Free Documentation License, Version 1.3.

First Printing: December 2015
Second Printing: June 2018

Master Books®, P.O. Box 726, Green Forest, AR 72638
Master Books® is a division of the New Leaf Publishing Group, Inc.

ISBN: 978-0-89051-866-3
ISBN: 978-1-61458-464-3 (digital)
Library of Congress Number: 2015950207

Cover illustration of Ancient Carthage by Bill Looney; see pages 59-62 for more information
Design by Diana Bogardus

Unless otherwise noted, Scripture quotations are from the New American Standard Version of the Bible.

Please consider requesting that a copy of this volume be purchased by your local library system.

Printed in China

Please visit our website for other great titles: www.masterbooks.com

For information regarding author interviews, please contact the publicity department at (870) 438-5288.

Master Books®
A Division of New Leaf Publishing Group
www.masterbooks.com

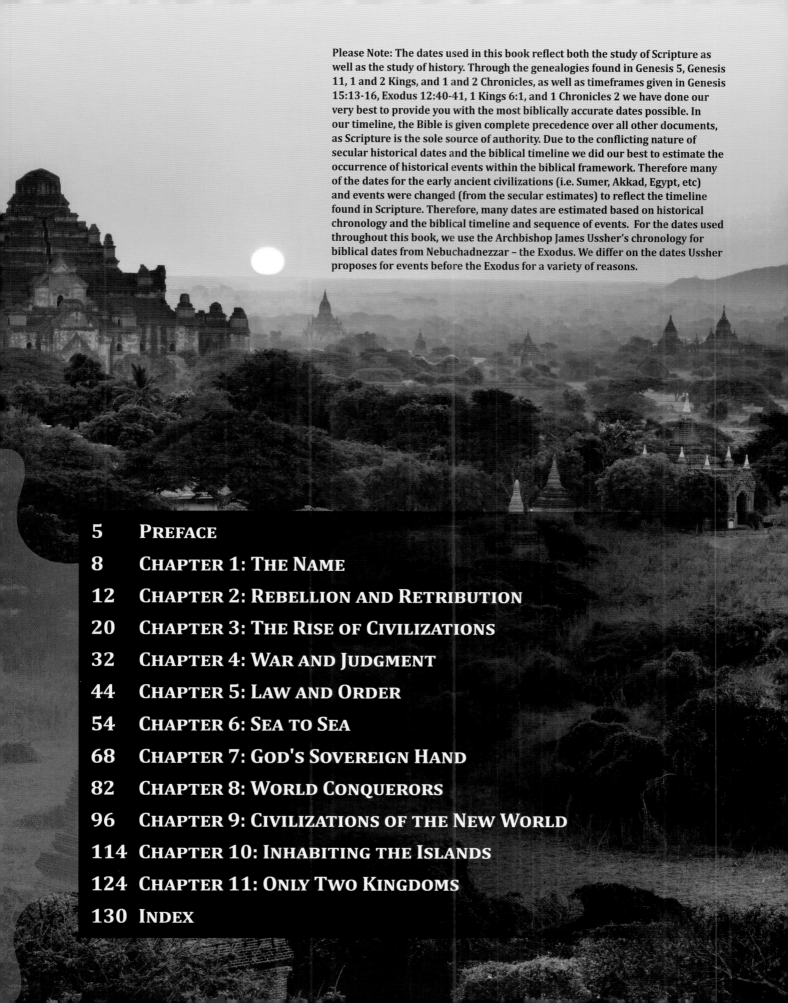

Please Note: The dates used in this book reflect both the study of Scripture as well as the study of history. Through the genealogies found in Genesis 5, Genesis 11, 1 and 2 Kings, and 1 and 2 Chronicles, as well as timeframes given in Genesis 15:13-16, Exodus 12:40-41, 1 Kings 6:1, and 1 Chronicles 2 we have done our very best to provide you with the most biblically accurate dates possible. In our timeline, the Bible is given complete precedence over all other documents, as Scripture is the sole source of authority. Due to the conflicting nature of secular historical dates and the biblical timeline we did our best to estimate the occurrence of historical events within the biblical framework. Therefore many of the dates for the early ancient civilizations (i.e. Sumer, Akkad, Egypt, etc) and events were changed (from the secular estimates) to reflect the timeline found in Scripture. Therefore, many dates are estimated based on historical chronology and the biblical timeline and sequence of events. For the dates used throughout this book, we use the Archbishop James Ussher's chronology for biblical dates from Nebuchadnezzar – the Exodus. We differ on the dates Ussher proposes for events before the Exodus for a variety of reasons.

"Search me, O God, and know my heart; try me and know my anxious thoughts; and see if there be any hurtful way in me, and lead me in the everlasting way."

—Psalm 139:23–24

PREFACE

Today you hold in your hands book two of a project that has engaged us for over five years. We never could have imagined the blessing it was to us to write *The Genius of Ancient Man*, and we are amazed and humbled by how God has used our first book. Our Ancient Man Research Team is passionate about this subject and we have been hard at work researching and writing new material since the publishing of *Genius.* We are thrilled about the opportunities we have been given through this second book. We want to share what God has laid on our hearts concerning the sinful rebellion of mankind, a rebellion that began in ancient times and has progressed through the centuries and into today.

In this book we have two main goals. One is to bring you more of the fascinating details you loved about ancient man, confirming his incredible intelligence and the spread of the common characteristics of Babel.

Our second goal is to draw your attention to the third purpose of Satan at the Tower of Babel: the call to "make a name." Often overlooked, this name-building effort became a rebellious worldview that is woven into the civilizations of ancient history. We will discover that this philosophy (values and motivations) of Babel still influences our world today and will continue into the future.

Remember that a "**worldview**" is the lens through which someone views and interacts with the things that happen in life. It is not a new concept; we all function in accordance with our worldview, as mankind has done from the beginning.

You will be reading a lot about Babel (or Babylon) in this book and you may find yourself wondering why this name keeps coming up. We use the term "Babel" or "Babel-influenced" to define and label the rebellious, humanistic worldview of mankind. We recognize that man's rebellion began in the garden, rose to a height before the flood and then was judged (and Satan's rebellion was even earlier). Yet this was not the end, and at Babel something unique happened: the whole world came together with a specific and clearly articulated purpose that has since been seemingly more discreet. The builders at Babel were openly rebelling against God and pursuing their own desires and goals, directly in an effort to usurp God's authority.

Babel was a climactic event and we believe the effects of that rebellion can be seen both physically around the world and also symbolically. So we use the term "Babel" to identify the humanistic philosophy that characterizes all of mankind's sin and rebellion. It is fascinating to track the characteristics of the "Babel-influenced" worldview and recognize the same things happening over and over again, all over the world in different cultures, languages and geographic locations.

We don't want this to be just another history book. We believe that history is so much more than mere facts and data, because we believe it was planned and orchestrated by a good and gracious God who has a purpose in all that He does. From the Bible, we know without a doubt that God created this earth, and mankind upon it, to bring Himself glory.

Bagan, Myanmar — one of the 2,200 Buddhist stupas or pagodas that remain from the original 10,000

Yet, as we described in *The Genius of Ancient Man*, there are two kingdoms at work in our world — God's and Satan's. Satan has been constantly at work preventing mankind from returning to God and enticing man deeper into his own counterfeit kingdom. His kingdom is characterized by the man-centered rebellious worldview that we believe is traceable in every civilization.

We hope to intrigue and fascinate you as we present the motivating factors and beliefs that influenced the civilizations throughout world history. We see that looking back, the worldview of the ancient peoples seems to be mirrored in the belief systems of the present, and we believe these same philosophical ideals will also have great influence in the future.

The Bible Teaches that all mankind has been stuck believing this rebellious worldview, but that there is also hope to be rescued from the "lusts of our flesh":

> "And you were dead in your trespasses and sins, in which you formerly walked according to the course of this world,

according to the prince of the power of the air, of the spirit that is now working in the sons of disobedience. Among them we too all formerly lived in the lusts of our flesh, indulging the desires of the flesh and of the mind, and were by nature children of wrath, even as the rest" (Ephesians 2:1–3).

Even the secular world recognizes that mankind has been motivated by similar values and beliefs throughout time:

> Whoever wishes to foresee the future must consult the past; for human events ever resemble those of preceding times. This arises from the fact that they are produced by men who ever have been, and ever shall be, animated by the same passions, and thus they necessarily have the same results. — Niccolo Machiavelli[1]

Therefore, as you read you should recognize aspects of popular worldviews of today and maybe even discover that your own worldview has been affected by ancient philosophy.

1   "Learning from History," http://www.age-of-the-sage.org/philosophy/history/learning_from_history.html, accessed January 26, 2013.

We have written this book to engage your mind. We have written it to challenge your thinking and to touch your heart. We live in a Babel-influenced world, a world that is a battleground between two authorities, a world that is constantly enticing you to stray from the truth and seek after worldly pleasures instead of glorifying God.

We invite you to join us as we again take you back in time. We invite you to think critically and to search for the sinful worldview that we talked about. As you read about the intriguing ancient civilizations, remember that they were populated with real people with thoughts and opinions, beliefs and influences; they had their own diverse cultures and religions, but they were really no different from us. Try to see beyond the ancient year in which they lived and look for the characteristics and motivating passions of their society that are mirrored in our own.

As you read, we pray that God will open your eyes to see the counterfeit of Satan's kingdom and the characteristics of Babel throughout history, and how they are even here today. Perhaps you will even see how his distortions may have influenced your own life.

chapter 1

Knowledge. Wisdom. Understanding. Mankind yearns for these. We find ourselves enthralled with secrets, mysteries, and riddles. Man is seduced by the unknown and enticed by the offer of revelation. Perhaps this is why we pursue science so passionately and we seek desperately to unearth the remnants of our ancestors. It is seen in our religions, literature, philosophy, and art, and evidenced by our exploration of earth, the moon, and deep space. We have this innate impression that there is something we don't know, something important that we must discover, something more to life than this.

Knowledge

God created mankind as finite beings, but Adam and Eve originally had a close relationship with the *infinite* Creator. He was the source of all the knowledge that they had, He was the lawgiver and provider of their needs. Yet an unavoidable characteristic of finite beings is ignorance. To be finite is to lack understanding and information that the infinite, by definition, must have. And to be finite is to be always learning more and adding to what knowledge has been acquired. God created mankind to desire knowledge and with the capability to obtain it, but He also created us to trust Him, and to trust that He has provided us with all we need to know.

For Adam and Eve, even while living in the splendor of God's undefiled creation, even with the opportunity to talk to the infinite God, Satan was able use their finiteness to tempt them with knowledge that they didn't have. Satan offered god-like status simply through acquiring knowledge — they would be *like* their Creator if only they *knew* more.

Adam and Eve were confronted with the reality of their own limited knowledge, in contrast to the all-knowing mind of God. Perhaps they were offended that God was withholding something from them.

Perhaps their pride told them that they deserved to be equal with God. Perhaps it was just the human fascination with the mysterious unknown, the "what ifs" and the "why nots" that we all ache to answer. For whatever the reason, Satan made them the offer, a way to get beyond their mere humanity; the opportunity was right there in front of them. Reach out, taste, and know. . . .

Ever since, Satan has been offering, tempting, and luring mankind to fulfill their desire to know. Yet the result of his offer never satisfies. It leaves us feeling even emptier than ever and more desperate to find the answers.

What is at the root of this desire? Why is the temptation so successful?

Power

It is our human pride that entices us (James 1:14). It is Satan's lie that on our own, we can achieve something. By offering man knowledge, he is offering power and authority.

In *The Genius of Ancient Man* we introduced you to the idea of "two kingdoms": there are only two religions, two kingdoms, and two authorities in the world. It is the two authorities that we want to draw your attention to in this book. The battle for authority has been raging since the Garden of Eden, between God's authority and man's perceived authority, offered by Satan. At the core of our sinful beings, in our pride, we believe that we have the right to authority over ourselves and even in many cases, over others.

It is interesting to note how often authority and power are connected to knowledge. Our pride provokes us to know more, to have understanding and wisdom. Our quest for knowledge is often self-centered and usually rebellious against God. This is not to say that knowledge is evil, or that it

View from the top of Borobudur Temple Compound located in Central Java in Indonesia.

is inherently wrong to search for knowledge and to yearn for discovery. God wants us to seek wisdom (Proverbs 2:1–6) and to eagerly learn about His creation! But when the search for knowledge does not lead us to worship God and further His glory, then it is wrong.

We are sinful beings, eagerly pursuing our own desires. We choose to reject God and pursue knowledge on our own, for our own purposes. We choose to establish our own authority and trust in man rather than our Maker. As Isaiah proclaimed, "All of us like sheep have gone astray, each of us has turned to his own way" (53:6). We have exchanged the truth of God for a lie; we worship and serve the creation instead of the Creator (Romans 1:25). It has been the tale of human history for thousands of years.

PURPOSE

These characteristics make up the man-centered philosophy that was established as a collective mindset at the Tower of Babel. The goal to "make a name" was rooted in human pride and

accomplishment. It was the epitome of rejecting God, very similar to Adam and Eve's sin. Just as in the Garden, at Babel mankind decided that they could rely on themselves. They rejected the authority of God, His kingship, His protection, and His standards. In their attempt to make a name for themselves, they rebelled against God and His provision. Mankind has been searching and grasping in darkness ever since.

And just as they did not see fit to acknowledge God any longer, God gave them over to a depraved mind, to do those things which are not proper, being filled with all unrighteousness, wickedness, greed, evil; full of envy, murder, strife, deceit, malice; they are gossips, slanderers, haters of God, insolent, arrogant, boastful, inventors of evil, disobedient to parents, without understanding, untrustworthy, unloving, unmerciful; and although they know the ordinance of God, that those who practice such things are worthy of death, they not only do the same, but also give hearty approval to those who practice them (Romans 1:28–32).

When man rebels against God and makes himself the authority, he is left trying to find meaning, purpose, and value starting from himself. But because man is finite and frail, unstable, and sinful, the conclusion of all his searching will be unsure, insecure, and will always come up empty.

Silver tetradachm owl coin — symbol of Athena, Greek goddess of wisdom

that His perfect, infallible Word, the Bible, is complete truth and speaks authoritatively over our lives. We believe the Bible takes priority over all other historical accounts, sciences, and persons.

Because of this, we know that history began "in the beginning" with the creation of the whole world in six days. Adam and Eve were the very first human beings, created on the sixth day in the very image of God: intelligent, creative, and without sin.

A History of Rebellion

As we study history in this book, we will be looking for the motivating factors that influenced the ancient world. We will find ourselves questioning and wondering about the unknowns and mysteries that time has hidden. Speculating about the past can be enticing and intriguing, but it can also be dangerous. We may find ourselves stumbling into areas of fiction without even realizing it. History is an intricate web of cultures, persons, influences, and events that intersect, disrupt, and intrude upon each other in confusing patterns. Interpretations of the web vary depending on which thread you are following. It can be easy for speculation to become fact in our own minds and in our presentation of it, even if we don't have definitive evidence. We must be wary of this.

All of our interpretations are also influenced by our *presuppositions*, the predetermined set of beliefs that we all have and that we assume to be true. These presuppositions are closely tied to our worldview and therefore influence everything we think and do. Presuppositions aren't necessarily wrong, but it is important to acknowledge their existence and to make sure that our presuppositions are indeed true.

When we (the authors of this book) study history and ancient man, we presuppose the existence of God. He is our starting point. We also believe

Until the Fall

When Adam and Eve chose to trust Satan and their own reason instead of submitting to God's authority, they set the course of history into the downward spiral that we have found ourselves in today. Sin has wreaked havoc on the world, its cultures and civilizations, practices and philosophies. We cannot ignore the presence of sinful rebellion when we study history. Mankind's rejection of God has been a motivating influence for thousands of years, and identifying that rebellion will help us to untangle some of the events and beliefs of the past.

There is so much insight and value to be gained from looking at the big picture of history, from start to present. Though this book won't touch on every nation, we have made every effort to study each of the major civilizations and to track what we believe is the most powerful motivator of mankind — his self-centered rebellion against God.

chapter 2

"Come, let us build for ourselves a city, and a tower whose top will reach into heaven, and let us make for ourselves a name . . ."

—Genesis 11:4

REBELLION AND RETRIBUTION

BABEL

[2402 B.C.]

For the purposes of this book we will be starting our record of human history at the civilization that came together at Babel. Though we acknowledge that history truly began much earlier at the creation of the world, since we have very little information about this time period due to the Flood, we will jump forward to roughly 2400 B.C. and the gathering at Babel. What began at this city was the first post-Flood blatant display of man's universal anti-God rebellion. As you will see, it was only the beginning of a world movement.

BUILDING A COUNTERFEIT

In the years after the Flood, Noah's descendants journeyed to and settled in the land of Shinar, literally meaning "between two rivers."[1] From the biblical account (Genesis 11:1–9) we know that it was in Shinar that the people came together and organized their rebellion against God. Their efforts and goals to build a city, tower, and name were initiated by a desire to defy God and His will. God had commanded the people to scatter and fill the earth, but they deliberately disobeyed this command, uniting under a new set of goals, in order to thwart God's purpose.

BABEL'S CALL

There are three aspects of the counterfeit that stand out as the chief elements of rebellion. The text of Genesis 11 defines them as *a city*, *a tower*, and *a name*.

From further study we can identify those elements as *political*, *religious*, and *philosophical* — the basis of the three-fold mission of Satan.

"COME, LET US" The goal of Babel was *unity*. It brought mankind together, against God's direct command to fill the earth, and gave them a sense of security and authority. They were united with one language and one purpose (Genesis 11:6), and this gave them immense strength and ability.

"BUILD A CITY" The city signifies that the people had political goals. They were organized, and the concept of unity carries the idea of one-world government. This concept has driven countless world powers throughout history to attempt world domination.

"A TOWER INTO HEAVEN" At Babel, the goal was to use their tower to reach into the heavens. It seems to have had very religious purposes because heaven is seen as the dwelling place of God (later, pyramids, monuments, and towers were usually built for religious reasons as well). Satan's counterfeit kingdom offers man the ability to be "like God," so the tower was probably their effort to design and manifest their own ability to be god — to enter the heavens themselves.

"A NAME FOR OURSELVES" The concept of "making a name" was the builders' approach to starting a new way of thinking. It was a system of belief in man, founded in mankind's abilities, his wisdom, his inventions, his discovery, and his reason.

---

1   Bodie Hodge, *Tower of Babel* (Green Forest, AR: Master Books, 2012), p. 46.

Through this philosophy, founded in pride, they would propose to find purpose, value, and meaning in life. It effectively removed the need for God and defined their worldview in entirely humanistic ideals.

The significance of this specific goal is often missed because it is not common knowledge that God gave names a great deal of importance. A name usually carried a lot more meaning and purpose in ancient times than we would expect in our Western culture.

What's in a Name?

Consider the Ten Commandments; when God gave Moses the law. The third commandment concerned the honor due His name. There is glorious weight and meaning instilled in the name of God. God introduced Himself to mankind through revelation of truth, by giving us first one, then two, then a whole sequence of names for Himself.

Each of God's names gives us more understanding of His nature, character, and attributes, and more information about Him — they are descriptions and unique characteristics. His names tell us who He is and what He is like. Thus, to take His name in vain, to misuse it or dishonor it, is to attack that quality of Himself conveyed by the name — it attacks His very character.

Moreover, in the Bible, the giving of names signifies dominion; for instance, God named the stars and He also named Adam. God allocated some authority and responsibility to man: Adam named Eve, as well as all the animals. But Adam's was only delegated authority, since all authority is ultimately God's.

When man decided to "make a name" for himself at Babel, he was really declaring self-authority and self-dominion. To make a name would be to decide for themselves who they would be — to decide their own meaning and purpose. And of course, they hoped to make it a lasting name — to outlive their own lives by the power of their influence and legacy.

We believe this man-centered concept, what philosophers would call "humanism," is visible throughout the civilizations of mankind's history even before Babel. But Babel is a great illustration because this way of thinking was inherent in Babel's initiator (Satan), builders, and followers. If man could attain his own spiritual enlightenment and become "like God," then other philosophical concepts follow — concepts that raise man up as the measure of all things and the authority over himself. Because we can track the evidence of Babel throughout historical civilizations (in religion, monument-building, astrology, etc.) we can study this worldview as well.

WAS NIMROD THE LEADER OF BABEL?

The name *Nimrod* literally means "we will revolt."	The mission at Babel was to come together against God's commands. Nimrod could be named (by God's sovereignty) for his personal involvement in the rebellion at Babel.
Nimrod was a mighty hunter before/ against the LORD (Genesis 10:8-9)	"Mighty" means "manly, vigorous; hero, champion; angel." The Arabic equivalent means "one who magnifies himself, behaves proudly, a tyrant, who is bold, audacious."
	This phrase "mighty hunter" is grammatically connected with the beginning of his kingdom in verse ten, meaning his kingdom is a result of his "hunting." Thus, he was a hunter of men, perhaps a successful tyrant, trapping men by force into his new imperial kingdom.
Babel is part of Nimrod's kingdom.	Genesis 10:10 — "The beginning of [Nimrod's] kingdom was Babel and Erech and Accad and Calneh, in the land of Shinar."
	Kingdom means "dominion, kingdom; kingship, royal sovereignty; king."
Evidence from legends all around the world	"Nimrod" is known all around the world by different names (because of the different languages that spread out from Babel). These names point to a false man-god trinity of Nimrod, Tammuz, and Semiramis.
	Accounts of men like Gilgamesh and Sargon are surprisingly similar to the biblical account of Nimrod and his kingdom.

rians: for even Menetho, who wrote the Egyptian history, and Berosus, who collected the Chaldean monuments, and Mochus, and Hestiæus, and besides these, Hieronymus the Egyptian, and those who composed the Phenician history, agree to what I here say: Hesiod also, and Hecatæus, and Hellanicus, and Acusilaus; and besides these, Ephorus and Nicolaus relate, that the ancients lived a thousand years. But as to these matters, let every one look upon them as they think fit.

CHAP. IV.

Concerning the Tower of Babylon, and the Confusion of Tongues.

Now the sons of Noah were three; Shem, Japhet, and Ham, born one hundred years before the deluge. These first of all descended from the mountains into the plains, and fixed their habitation there; and persuaded others who were greatly afraid of the lower grounds on account of the flood, and so were very loath to come down from the higher places, to venture to follow their examples. Now the plain in which they first dwelt, was called *Shinar*. God also commanded them to send colonies abroad, for the thorough peopling of the earth, that they might not raise seditions among themselves, but might cultivate a great part of the earth, and enjoy its fruits after a plentiful manner. But they were so ill-instructed, that they did not obey God; for which reason they fell into calamities, and were made sensible by experience of what sin they had been guilty: for when they flourished with a numerous youth, God admonished them again to send out colonies; but they, imagining that the prosperity they enjoyed was not derived from the favour of God, but supposing that their own power was the proper cause of the plentiful condition they were in, did not obey him. Nay, they added to this their disobedience to the divine will, the suspicion that they were therefore ordered to send out separate colonies, that being divided asunder they might the more easily be oppressed.

Now it was Nimrod who excited them to such an affront and contempt of God. He was the grandson of Ham, the son of Noah, a bold man, and of great strength of hand. He persuaded them not to ascribe it to God, as if it was through his means they were happy, but to believe that it was their own courage which procured that happiness. He also gradually changed the government into tyranny, seeing no other way of turning men from the fear of God, but to bring them into a constant dependence on his power. He also said, "he would be revenged on God, if he should have a mind to drown the world again, for that he would build a tower too high for the water to be able to reach; and that he would avenge himself on God for destroying their forefathers."

Now the multitude were very ready to follow the determination of Nimrod, and to esteem it a piece of cowardice to submit to God; and they built a tower, neither sparing any pains, nor being in any degree

From *The Complete Works of Flavius Josephus* by William Whiston, A. M.; original printing circa-1850. Green Forest, AR: Master Books, 2008.

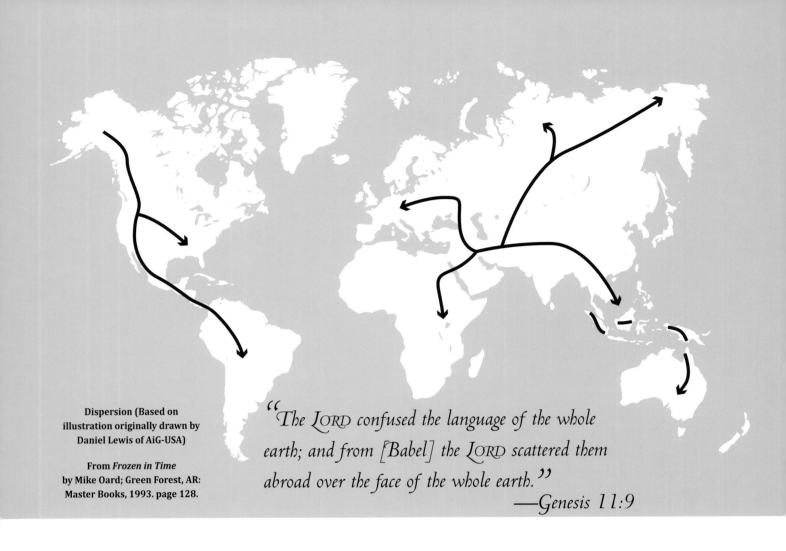

Dispersion (Based on illustration originally drawn by Daniel Lewis of AiG-USA)

From *Frozen in Time* by Mike Oard; Green Forest, AR: Master Books, 1993. page 128.

"The LORD confused the language of the whole earth; and from [Babel] the LORD scattered them abroad over the face of the whole earth."
—Genesis 11:9

THE BIRTH OF MANY CIVILIZATIONS

One of the most significant outcomes of the rebellion at Babel was God's judgment of their sin: He confused the languages and dispersed mankind across the globe.

The characteristics of Babel are subsequently woven into every civilization that arose after this dispersion and yet, each also has unique differences in development and timing. This is because, even though the people were not separated from their rebellious goals, they were divided from each other. The separation caused the creation of different cultures and people groups.

SCATTERED FROM BABEL
[2402 B.C.]

By using a combination of archaeological sciences, the different routes that the ancient people used on their journeys away from Babel can be roughly tracked. Though not everyone traveled extremely far distances, many did begin the journey to the far reaches of the earth and their routes were greatly influenced by the changing climate as the Ice Age developed. The cooler temperatures made travel through the north more difficult due to the build-up of the ice caps, but the lower ocean levels would have exposed more land for travel and allowed the people to cross into areas that would become more isolated later.

The environmental fluctuations led to four distinct routes that the people could have taken:

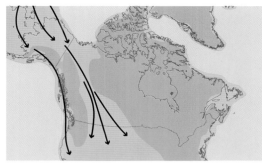

Southwest to Palestine and Africa	Due to the Ice Age causing cooler temperatures around the globe, there would have been more precipitation in the mid-latitude regions, meaning the areas that are deserts today would have been cooler and wetter. Even the Sahara would remain a fertile and habitable place long after the Flood!
Southeast to India, Asia, and the Pacific Islands	Even with the mountain ranges and small stretches of ocean in the way of this route, it would have been an easier trip than the route up into the north.
Northwest to Europe and Northern Asia	The same aftereffects of the Flood that made the south a tropical paradise made the north a harsh, cold landscape. As the Ice Age progressed, the immigrants would be met with the advancing ice sheets. Days were darker and the seasons much colder.

When the people scattered, they would have divided according to their new languages. (We do not know the size of these groups; most believe they could have been divided by family.) These new language groups would have taken their own share of civilization-building knowledge (including politics, religion, skills, education, etc.) from the Tower of Babel and carried that with them wherever they went. This would have contributed to the differences we observe among the varying cultures.

Also note, the migration did not have to happen in one continuous burst. Populations could have moved along at a leisurely pace, following herds of game while they needed to and settling down when they found a promising piece of land. Years later, a younger generation could pick up and migrate farther, again taking their intelligence and abilities with them.

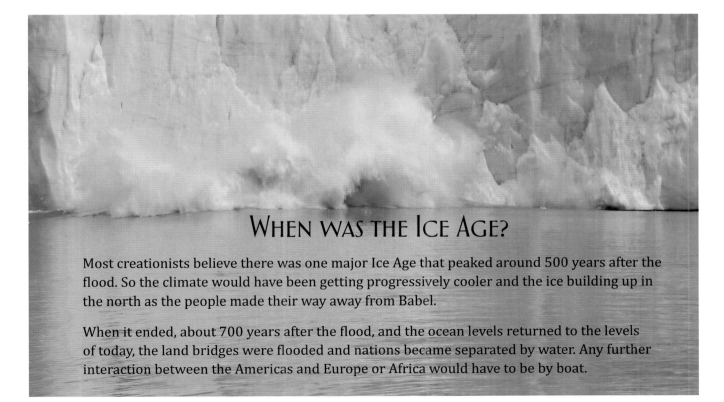

When was the Ice Age?

Most creationists believe there was one major Ice Age that peaked around 500 years after the flood. So the climate would have been getting progressively cooler and the ice building up in the north as the people made their way away from Babel.

When it ended, about 700 years after the flood, and the ocean levels returned to the levels of today, the land bridges were flooded and nations became separated by water. Any further interaction between the Americas and Europe or Africa would have to be by boat.

OVER LAND

It makes sense that ancient man would have traveled through valleys and over mountains to reach areas like Africa, Europe, and Asia, but what about reaching a more remote landmass like North and South America? Is it possible they simply walked over? Actually, yes, this is a very plausible and accepted theory. The most likely route ancient man could have taken to get to North America would be across the Bering Strait while it was exposed during the Ice Age. There were also possible land bridges through southeast Asia to Australia.

Bering Strait

OVER SEA

It is likely that the ancient people traveled by boat to different locations as well. Evidence of ancient seafaring explains the populations on Pacific islands and people groups in South America like the Olmec.

It may seem obvious, but we often need reminding that these people were the descendants of the great shipbuilder Noah and his three sons. The knowledge required to craft boats would have naturally been passed on to younger generations and carried across the globe, just like the knowledge of religion, farming, and city building, etc.

HOW LONG DID IT TAKE?

There is no reason to believe that this incredible journey was impossible within a biblical time frame.

Michael Oard states in his book *Frozen in Time*:

> The journey from the Tigris-Euphrates Rivers to the southern tip of South America did not need to be a grueling journey, as some have envisioned, nor did it need to take a long time. If the tribes were nomadic hunters and they averaged two miles a day for only four of the warmest months, they would move at the rate of 250 miles (400 km) a year. The distance to the southern tip of South America is about 15,000 miles (24,000 km). At the rate of 250 miles (400 km) each SUMMER, the people could have made the journey in only 60 years.[1]

Sixty years would be the speedy minimum; the people were probably moving much slower than this, but it does put things into perspective.

Having mankind divided into languages was a judgment from God, but that did not prevent Him from using the event to His glory. He had originally commanded Noah's family to spread out and fill the earth, and even though the people tried to come together against this command, as always, God's will and purpose prevailed. Our beautifully diverse peoples, languages, and cultures are a direct result of this event.

Ever wondered why certain civilizations took longer than others to become well established? As you will learn in this book, the Middle East, Northern Africa,

1   Michael Oard, *Frozen in Time* (Green Forest, AR: Master Books, 2004) http://www. answersingenesis.org/articles/fit/man-during-ice-age.

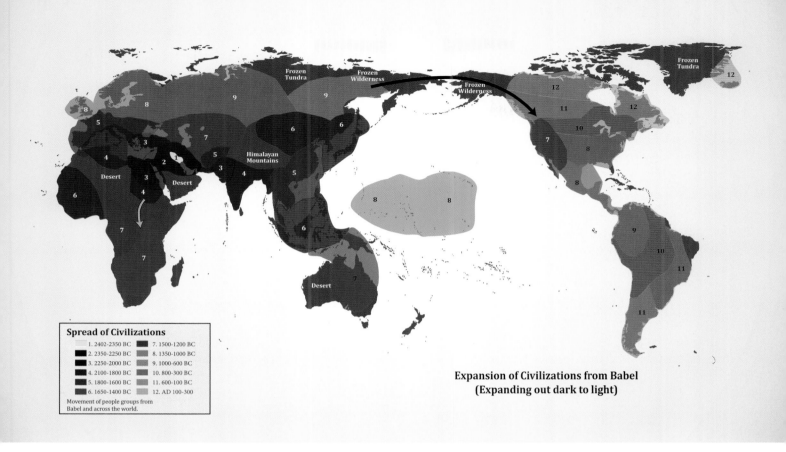

Expansion of Civilizations from Babel
(Expanding out dark to light)

Spread of Civilizations

1. 2402-2350 BC		7. 1500-1200 BC	
2. 2350-2250 BC		8. 1350-1000 BC	
3. 2250-2000 BC		9. 1000-600 BC	
4. 2100-1800 BC		10. 800-300 BC	
5. 1800-1600 BC		11. 600-100 BC	
6. 1650-1400 BC		12. AD 100-300	

Movement of people groups from Babel and across the world.

and Europe rose to greatness literally thousands of years before the Americas, Australia, and Africa!

By looking at history, we can track how the civilizations spread from Babel. The people who stayed in the Middle East quickly established cities after the Dispersion and continued to progress at a rapid rate. The Indus Valley and some European areas were settled shortly thereafter, followed by China. It took much longer for those traveling all the way to Australia, Southern Africa, and the Americas to develop any significant civilizations.

The outer reaches of the globe would have had a much later population growth because the people had to travel farther and were spread thinly over a vast geographical area.

Isolation also played a major part in the slower advancement of the Americas, Southern Africa, and Australia. In the Middle East, Northern Africa, and Europe, the people could easily trade supplies as well as ideas and technology. In more remote places, the people were isolated and cut off from the rest of the world. This limited the amount of information that could be shared and handed down. They were

not less intelligent; they simply had less people, less information, and it took them much longer to reach their final destination. All these things resulted in much slower growth.

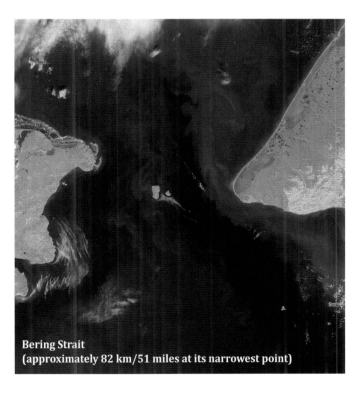

Bering Strait
(approximately 82 km/51 miles at its narrowest point)

chapter 3

THE RISE OF CIVILIZATIONS

WHAT MAKES A "CIVILIZATION"?

It's one of the words that will be coming up often in this book, and yet its meaning can be somewhat vague. Merriam-Webster defines "civilization" this way:

a: a relatively high level of cultural and technological development; specifically: the stage of cultural development at which writing and the keeping of written records is attained

b: the culture characteristic of a particular time or place[1]

Generally speaking, we will be using the word to describe a group of people, similar to a nation. A civilization has a cohesive, organized structure and recognizable characteristics that set it apart from others.

Civilizations don't necessarily have exact dates for their existence but rather approximate time periods in which they rose and fell. They often overlapped each other, even in the same region, as one people group rose in the wake of another.

Among the oldest civilizations known to post-Flood history is Sumer. It rose quickly after the dispersion of Babel due to its close geographic proximity. Since these people chose to resettle the immediate area, they didn't have to spend many years traveling before establishing their nation.

Sumer is credited with the invention of writing systems, the first law codes, the first large organized cities, the first kingship, and the first empire. (An empire is usually defined as an extensive territory, or number of territories all ruled by one entity.)

SUMER
[2350–2300 B.C.]

The ancient civilization of Sumer was organized into city-states; each city maintained its own ruler and protected its own borders, but they were still aligned with each other in interest. All of the cities had the same religious system and pantheon of gods,[2] but each city usually claimed a "patron" god that they worshiped above all others. Each city's ruler was concerned about protecting the reputation and honor of its patron god. [3,4]

While there were several important cities within the Sumerian civilization, we will focus on the great city of Erech (spelled "Uruk" by many historians).

ERECH

Erech is considered the oldest city in the world by a vast majority of historians. While their timeline is incorrect due to their evolutionary worldview, we believe it is one of the first cities to be constructed, built soon after the dispersion of Babel. The city was supposedly founded by the legendary king, Gilgamesh, from the famous myth The *Epic of Gilgamesh*.

The ancient story is thought to be based on a real, historical king however, there is a great deal of fiction mixed in with the facts. We cannot place too much authority on a legend, but it is important to remember that most mythology does contain at least a small amount of truth — the key is to

2   A pantheon is a set of all the gods of a particular religion, mythology, or tradition.
3   Mark, Joshua J. "Sumer." Ancient History Encyclopedia. April 28, 2011. Accessed May 6, 2015. http://www.ancient.eu/sumer/.
4   Guisepi, Robert A., and F. Roy Willis. "Sumeria, Ancient Sumeria (Sumer), A History of Ancient Sumer Including Its Contributions." Accessed May 6, 2015. http://history-world.org/sumeria.htm

1   "Civilization," http://www.merriam-webster.com/dictionary/civilization.

see if it is contradicted by more reliable sources (particularly the Bible). According to Scripture, Erech was indeed among the first cities built after the Flood. In Genesis 10:10 it is listed as one of the beginning cities of Nimrod's kingdom.

Erech was apparently famous for its massive "impenetrable" walls. The *Epic* claims that they were built using pre-Flood knowledge. The fabled walls stretched over six miles in circumference around the city.

The city itself was a marvel; it included a variety of large structures including platforms, temples, ziggurats, and cemeteries. Astonishingly, it covers almost 1,000 acres, making it by far the largest city in the world at the time. It became the capital city of several civilizations, starting with the Sumerians and then the Akkadians and later the Babylonians. Its prominence slowly declined as other cities were favored due to better trade locations, but it remained populated until the first century A.D.[5]

Erech is a great example of ancient people engineering far greater architecture than is typically believed. The walls of Erech were just as formidable and impressive as civilizations that arose far later in history (i.e. Babylon, Jerusalem, Constantinople, etc.). The well-structured political and religious branches are evidence affirming the intelligence of the ancient Sumerian citizens.

A general view of the Uruk archaeological site at Warka in Iraq. The site of Uruk was discovered in 1849 by William Kennett Loftus, who led the first excavations from 1850 to 1854. The Arabic name of Babylonia, al-ʿIrāq, is thought to be derived from the name Uruk, via Aramaic (Erech) and possibly Middle Persian (Erāq) transmission.

5   Mark, Joshua J. "Uruk." Ancient History Encyclopedia. April 28, 2011. Accessed May 6, 2015. http://www.ancient.eu/uruk/.

Epic of Gilgamesh

The *Epic of Gilgamesh* is fascinating not only because it associates the hero Gilgamesh with the building of a real historical city, but because it has more interesting information that could also be true. We must be careful with this text because it definitely contains a lot of embellishment and fiction, but it is intriguing to dig through looking for shreds of truth.

In the *Epic of Gilgamesh* there are several pieces of information that provide insight into events that did indeed take place according to Scripture. First, the *Epic* makes many references to a global flood. One section is entirely dedicated to describing this massive catastrophic event.

It describes the tale of Utnapishtim, who was told by one of the gods that a flood was coming. He built a boat to carry him, his family, and a male and female of every kind of animal to safety. This tale corresponds with many other myths, such as the Atra-Hasis, which originated from the Akkadians and Babylonians.[6]

Many believe that the *Epic* is the oldest poem in existence and is therefore the source of all the other flood stories. However, we know that Scripture, as the Word of God, has priority over all other documents. The source of the flood legends is the global flood itself, not a mythical story. The flood story in the *Epic* is just a distorted version of what really happened, as described in the Bible.[7]

The Great Mystery

Another interesting aspect of this legend is the actual person of "Gilgamesh." The *Epic* states that Gilgamesh was the genius behind the great walls constructed at Erech and that he used pre-Flood knowledge to build them. It describes his vast knowledge by saying he had "seen the great Mystery and knew the hidden" and that he "recovered the knowledge of all the times before

Hero mastering a lion. Relief from the façade of the throne room, Palace of Sargon II at Khorsabad (Dur-Sharrukin), ca. 713–706 B.C.

6   Mark, Joshua J. "Sargon of Akkad." Ancient History Encyclopedia. September 2, 2009. Accessed May 6, 2015. http://www.ancient.eu/Sargon_of_Akkad/.
7   Mark, Joshua J. "The Atrahasis Epic: The Great Flood and the Meaning of Suffering." Ancient History Encyclopedia. March 6, 2011. Accessed May 6, 2015. http://www.ancient.eu/article/227/.

the Flood."[8] In the *Epic,* the walls are honored because of this unique knowledge.

But what does the text mean by "hidden" and "the great Mystery"? Why is pre-Flood knowledge held in such high regard? Why is it significant in the building of the walls of Erech?

We believe pre-Flood man would have been brilliant and probably had incredible building and technological skills. Ever since Adam and Eve's sin, mankind has been on a downward spiral due to the effects of sin and the Curse; it is logical to assume that the people from before the Flood were far more intelligent than we are today because they were less affected by the degrading results of the Curse. With their incredibly long lifespans, it makes sense that they would be among the most accomplished people to ever live.

It didn't take very long for post-Flood people to begin utilizing whatever knowledge Noah's family was able to preserve through the Flood. This explains why they already knew how to build large, planned structures and cities, how they rapidly began farming with irrigation, and how they were able to craft metal tools and weapons. They didn't have to rediscover these skills.

Now don't mistake our meaning here, we are not trying to say that pre-Flood civilizations had more advanced technology than we currently have today. We are however stating that they were likely more intelligent and skilled. The reason we have more advanced technology today is because we have had 6,000 years to build up a vast amount of knowledge; once that base is achieved, you start to see amazing advances in technological inventions. And yet, even with our great advantage, we still cannot understand how the ancient people did certain things.

So is the *Epic* merely referring to the great skill and knowledge of the people before the Flood? Or was there something else mysterious and hidden that he had access to? The text of the *Epic* does not give us these answers.

Akkadian text from the Deluge tablet of the Gilgamesh epic

THE QUEST FOR IMMORTALITY

The *Epic of Gilgamesh* not only gives us a retelling of the Flood and information about a legendary hero, but the entire tale actually focuses on and leads up to one aspect of Gilgamesh's life that links him to Babel: his pursuit of immortality and godhood.

The story follows the life of Gilgamesh, the great hero, as he goes on an adventure that leads to the death of one of his friends. It is this death that compels him on a quest to achieve immortality. He gets "close" to this goal twice, but he is thwarted both times. In the first attempt, Utnapishtim, the man who survived the Flood, told him that if he never slept again, he would be granted immortality. Unfortunately, after a long time, Gilgamesh slept for seven days and thus lost his chance.

His second attempt required him to fetch a rare plant that would make him young again from the bottom of a river. Upon its retrieval, a snake stole it from him.

After these two foiled attempts, Gilgamesh returned to the city of Erech and there realized his only real chance at immortality. Gilgamesh discerned a way to make sure that he was remembered forever. He pointed to his famous walls and proclaimed that through them, his greatest achievement, he would be immortal and never forgotten.

---

8   *The Epic of Gilgamesh.* Translation by Yanita Chen, 1994.

A Common Pursuit

It is a common theme in many mythologies across the globe: heroes being rewarded with the ultimate gift of immortality and/or godhood. Many of the heroes in ancient myths sought to conquer death, whether for themselves or for the ones they loved. If you read many legends or watch many fantasy films, you will have noticed this trend.

But have you ever stopped to ponder where this desire came from originally? Have you ever connected the pursuit for immortality and godhood to the original sin of Adam and Eve? Satan offered them the same thing: they would not die but rather be "like God" if they ate from the tree.

This prideful desire has been a driving force for many of the great kings throughout history. Many even claimed godhood and required their people to worship them, such as Alexander the Great, the Egyptian pharaohs, some of the Roman caesars, and Nebuchadnezzar.

When we come to legends and myths like the *Epic of Gilgamesh,* we can clearly see the connection to Babel — it has the same philosophy. Gilgamesh attempted to achieve physical immortality and, while he failed, he settled for second best: to be remembered forever for his achievements. Almost every great ruler has come to the same realization — the only way for them to gain some kind of immortality is to achieve great things.

Leaders Who Claimed Godhood	
Gilgamesh (Sumer)	Descendant of the gods/part god
Hammurabi (Babylon)	Messenger of the gods
Ramses II (Egypt)	Put himself at the same level as the greatest Egyptian gods (all pharaohs claimed to be descended from the sun god, Ra)
Nebuchadnezzar (Babylon)	"Is this not Babylon the great, which I myself have built as a royal residence by the might of my power and for the glory of my majesty?" (Daniel 4:30)
Qin Shi Huang Di (China)	Chinese emperors were deified as "Sons of Heaven" since the Qin dynasty
Alexander the Great (Greece)	Claimed to be descended from Zeus
Augustus and Julius Caesar (Rome)	Augustus deified Julius Caesar and then called himself "Son of the Divine One"
Nero (Rome)	Claimed godhood
Caligula (Rome)	Claimed godhood

Akkad

[2300–2100 B.C.]

The civilization of Akkad was named after one of its great cities. The city of Akkad was among the first to be built after the Dispersion and was originally part of the Sumerian empire. Its exact location has yet to be discovered (but it is one of the cities named in Genesis 10:10). Whereas Sumer is credited with being the first post-Flood civilization, Akkad rose up to become the first conquering empire, defeating and taking control of many cities. One man, now known as Sargon the Great, led Akkad into preeminence and power.

Sargon the Great was the first significant conqueror in recorded history. He supposedly came from humble beginnings as a mere gardener, yet eventually he rose in prominence and rank and was able to gain control of military troops in the city of Akkad, which was still part of Sumer at the time. Through political and military means he quickly rose in power over the city of Akkad and began to overthrow the neighboring cities. He eventually took control of most of the Sumerian empire by defeating Lugalzaggisi, who was ruling at the time. Sargon then set his sights on the rest of Mesopotamia and started taking control of the cities along the Euphrates River all the way to Syria. He went on to take over Susa (capital of the Elamites, later to be the capital of Assyria).

Sargon was revered as his reputation grew quickly. His fame and prowess as a warrior and leader became greater and greater, launching him into almost mythical status. According to legend, Sargon's mere presence was able to quell any dispute or rebellion. He went down in history as the greatest king of Akkad and the first great empire builder.

Sargon the Great was the first to attempt to reunite the world through military might, though many would follow his example later. His thirst for power was great and he was very skilled in leadership and organization.[9]

---

9   Mark, Joshua J. "Sargon of Akkad." Ancient History Encyclopedia. September 2, 2009. Accessed May 6, 2015. http://www.ancient.eu/Sargon_of_Akkad/.

Inscription of Naram-Sin, Sargon's grandson, telling the construction of the Marad temple by his own grandson Lipit-Ili circa 2250 B.C.

Was Sargon Actually Nimrod?

There are many fascinating similarities between the historical account of Sargon and Nimrod, described in Scripture.

Genesis 10:8 states: "Cush fathered Nimrod; he was the first on earth to be a mighty man" (ESV). This term "mighty man" means powerful, champion, chief, valiant, warrior, tyrant, and other similar words.

Genesis 10:10–12 describes the land Nimrod controlled: "The beginning of his kingdom was Babel and Erech and Accad and Calneh, in the land of Shinar. From that land he went forth into Assyria, and built Nineveh and Rehoboth-Ir and Calah, and Resen between Nineveh and Calah; that is the great city."

This land area is very similar to the land that Sargon controlled. Nimrod controlled four cities that were part of the kingdom of Sumer, which was the first place Sargon conquered. Nimrod then went into Assyria and built more cities there; once again, this corresponds with Sargon, who went and conquered Assyria only after he had control of Sumer.

Sargon's military effort to conquer and control the surrounding nations seems to have a similar characteristic to the goals of Babel — unity and one-world government. After the scattering from Babel, the rebellious people would be angry with God and still very determined to have their own way. Perhaps Sargon was still attempting to stop the dispersion of the people, this time by military might.

Why would he attempt this futile rebellion? For the same reason any man rebels against God: anger and rejection of the truth. Sargon would have known full well who God was, because Noah and his sons were still alive during his time! (If Sargon is really just another name for Nimrod, then Noah was his great-grandfather!) Instead of trusting in God he chose to rebel against Him again. While Sargon does bear some remarkable similarities to Nimrod, there is no way to tell for sure. As you read previously, Sargon's rise to power was not the same as Nimrod's (though nothing is really known about Nimrod's rise or early life), therefore he may have simply been one who was similar to Nimrod and his characteristics, but not Nimrod himself.

	known as ...	Beginning of Kingdom	Expansion/Conquest
Nimrod	a mighty man"	Babel, Erech, Accad, Calneh (Shinar/Sumer)	Nineveh, Rehoboth-Ir, Calah, Resen (Assyria)
Sargon	"the Great" — a legendary warrior and leader	Rose from city of Akkad and overthrew neighboring cities in Sumer/Shinar	Conquered cities along Euphrates and then conquered Susa (Assyria)

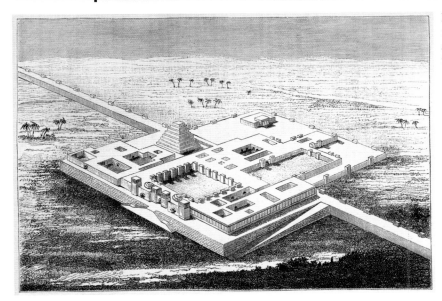

Palace of Khorsabad (Dur-Sharrukin) 1882, located in present-day Iraq and served as the Assyrian capital during the time of Sargon II of Assyria.

Gobekli Tepe in Turkey — a mysterious site that continues to amaze and confuse archaeologists and historians.

GOBEKLI TEPE

[APPROXIMATELY 2350–2200 B.C.]

Who's ready for some mystery? Gobekli Tepe is ancient ambiguity at its best! Mostly unknowns and fascinating questions, the people who constructed this site left a puzzling legacy that is still being uncovered in the semi-deserts of Turkey.

THE "NAVEL OF THE WORLD"

Gobekli Tepe means "Hill with a Belly" or "Navel Mound."[10] For generations, the locals have considered the nondescript, gently mounded hill to be a sacred site: the "navel of the world."

For years, researchers have been trying to uncover the mysteries of this site and now, through the use of ground-penetrating radar and geomagnetic surveys, what lies buried in the belly of the hill has been revealed: 20 megalithic stone-walled rings. Out of the 22 acres that make up Gobekli Tepe, only one acre of excavation — revealing four circles — has given us a physical glimpse of this site. Each of the rounded structures are similar — one circle is built within another and lined with towering T-shaped limestone blocks, each eight feet tall and weighing around seven tons. The pillars face inward to the center of the circle where the two tallest pillars

10   "Ancient Sites in Turkey," http://www.ancient-wisdom.co.uk/turkey.htm.

For the secular world, the idea that early Neolithic hunter-gatherers built something like this is world changing. They were not considered advanced enough. "It's like discovering that a three-year-old child made the Empire State Building out of toy bricks."[15]

But when we operate under the biblical presupposition that man was created in the image of God, highly intelligent and creative, around 6,000 years ago, sites like Gobekli Tepe are not shocking to find.

In fact, the term "hunter-gatherer" should not translate into "primitive." It's a lifestyle, oftentimes just a temporary one. People have lived according to this lifestyle throughout the years of history — they are not confined to a certain period and cannot be called "less intelligent" because of it.

The First Temple?

The construction at Gobekli Tepe likely started soon after the dispersion of the people from Babel (probably between 2350 and 2200 B.C.). The builders had traveled over 400 miles and probably adopted the hunter-gatherer lifestyle as they made their journey.

But why did they stop and build this amazing monument?

As we presented and confirmed through our research in *The Genius of Ancient Man*, the people who scattered from Babel regularly built mounds, pillars, pyramids, and monuments similar to their first impressive tower reaching into heaven. We have asserted that the tower building was motivated by religious and philosophical reasons, an anti-God rebellion that sought to make mankind the measure of all things.

So we believe that Gobekli Tepe is a monument built with those same motivating factors. Recall that Gobekli Tepe is not merely four stone circles;

stand (between 16 and 18 feet high).[11] The circular structures have durable terrazzo floors made from burnt limestone and clay, polished to give them a spotted appearance.[12]

Most of the limestone pillars are smooth and unadorned, but others bear the relief carvings of leopards and wild boars. Also depicted are a host of other creatures such as lions, foxes, vultures, snakes, and scorpions crawling over the stone. The images of herons and geese and the forms of men have been found as well.

This site has astounded archaeologists and shattered the previously held secular timeline for how ancient man evolved, because they date Gobekli Tepe at approximately 10,000–9,000 B.C., by secular means, the Early Neolithic time period.[13] According to secular science, this period was populated only by primitive hunter-gatherers.[14]

11 Andrew Curry, "Gobekli Tepe: The World's First Temple?" *Smithsonian Magazine*, November 2008, http://www.smithsonianmag.com/history/gobekli-tepe-the-worlds-first-temple-83613665.
12 David Smith, "Monuments at Gobekli Tepe — Overturning Expectations about Ancient Man," Answers, April–June 2014: p. 41–42.
13 "Gobekli — Site of Eden?" http://newphoenix.info/?p=2021.
14 Robert A. Guisepi, "An Overview of the Paleolithic," http://history-world.org/stone_age1.htm.
15 *National Geographic*, "Lost Civilization: Gobekli Tepe — 12,000 years ago," http://abaclips.com/info/lost-civilization-gobekli-tepe-12000-years-ago-part-25-national-geografic360p/KbKJsvFz0LpDEjA.html.

WHAT WERE THEY WORSHIPING?

Andrew Curry, in his article on Gobekli Tepe for *Smithsonian Magazine* in 2008, had this to say when confronted with interpreting Gobekli Tepe.

> Indeed, though I stood among the looming megaliths eager to take in their meaning, they didn't speak to me. They were utterly foreign, placed there by people who saw the world in a way I will never comprehend. There are no sources to explain what the symbols might mean.[17]

That, however, cannot stop the urge to explain the unexplainable; theories claiming to sum up Gobekli Tepe's hidden meaning abound. Schmidt refers to it as the "Temple of the Hunt" where the hunter-gatherers worshiped their gods, symbolized by the predators and prey etched upon the pillars. Others try to connect Gobekli Tepe with archaeoastronomy (aligning architecture according to astronomical events or objects). They propose that either the carvings on the pillars represent an ancient cosmology or the layout of the stone circles themselves is part of a geoglyph depicting a bull, with the stone circles representing the star cluster Pleiades within the constellation Taurus.[18]

it is a whole manmade hill full of buried circular structures.

Consider another factor: that the builders didn't actually *live* at this site. Archaeologist Klaus Schmidt rules out Gobekli Tepe as a dwelling place or village and states:

> Gobekli Tepe is not a house or a domestic building. Evidence of any domestic use is entirely lacking. No remains of settled human habitation have been found nearby. That leaves one purpose: religion.[16]

Mysterious depictions of animals are found within the Gobekli Tepe site.

---

16 Sean Thomas, "Paradise Regained," *ForteanTimes,* March 2007, http://www.forteantimes.com/features/articles/449/gobekli_tepe_paradise_regained.html, accessed September 28, 2014.

17 Curry, "Gobekli Tepe: The World's First Temple?"
18 Wayne Herschel, "Gobekli Tepe — Oldest Civilization on Earth . . . Deciphered!" http://thehiddenrecords.com/gobekli-tepe-taurus-bull.php.

Archaeoastronomy

One of the most outstanding examples displaying the intellect of ancient man is their knowledge of the heavens and astronomy. The study of ancient astronomical achievements is known as "archaeoastronomy."

Some of the most prominent and impressive examples of archaeoastronomy discovered so far include:

- Stonehenge
- The Pyramids of Giza

The City of Alexandria

Cahokia's Woodhenge

Ohio's Serpent Mound

Carnac, France

Some would say it is futile to attempt to discover the original purpose for this site. But is it? We can discern several important things from what we do know of Gobekli Tepe and what we know of Babel and human history. Viewed through the lens of Scripture, even more intriguing possibilities come to light.

First, the site is considered sacred and almost certainly has religious importance. Further, we know that the majority of the people dispersed at Babel took part in the rebellion against God.

What do we know about these builders in particular? The depiction of so many animals carved into their monument brings to mind a passage from Romans:

> [They] exchanged the glory of the incorruptible God for an image in the form of corruptible man and of birds and four-footed animals and crawling creatures. . . . For they exchanged the truth of God for a lie, and worshiped and served the creature rather than the Creator (Romans 1:23–25).

And another passage in which Ezekiel describes a vision from God seems to describe a similar scene:

> And He said to me, "Go in and see the wicked abominations that they [the elders of Israel] are committing here." So I entered and looked, and behold, every form of creeping things and beasts and detestable things, with all the idols of the house of Israel, were carved on the wall all around. (Ezekiel 8:9–10).

The location of their chosen site should also pique your interest. Gobekli Tepe is located at the *highest elevation* of the Germus mountain range overlooking the Harran plain.[19] The *man-made mound* that forms Gobekli Tepe makes the site even higher.

At first this ancient monument seems unique and bizarre, but it actually portrays some of the very same characteristics that later civilizations display: mound building, worship of creation rather than creator, archaeoastronomy, and a fascinating attraction toward mountains.

In an angry response to God, were these builders seeking to worship anything except the Judge who had confused their languages and scattered them? Instead of building a tower, did they find the highest point they could get toward the heavens and then build higher?

These questions lead us into the world of conjecture and theory, but the similarities and signs of the ancient rebellion are clear at Gobekli Tepe. Was this one of the first pagan temples to ever be built? It would confirm man's perseverance in pursuing his own goals and gods. Regardless of the commands and judgments of God, the builders organized themselves again and set up their own religion, an anti-God glorification of the animal kingdom.

---

19 "Turkey: Gobekli Tepe". World Archeology. (May 28, 2012). http://www.world-archaeology.com/features/turkey-gobekli-tepe.htm. Accessed September 9, 2014

chapter 4

WAR AND JUDGMENT

It was not long after the dispersion from Babel that incredibly advanced civilizations were already forming even beyond the Mesopotamian area. We know that the people were intelligent and skilled builders (they had worked together to build the city and Tower of Babel) and that for those who scattered nearby, it would not have taken long to build new cities and empires. These ancient cities show some of the most impressive works of mankind in ancient times.

MINOANS

[2150–1450 B.C. PEAK 1900–1600 B.C.]

The Minoan civilization was located on the island of Crete in the Mediterranean Sea, and is regarded today as one of the most advanced to be discovered. The technological accomplishments of their structures were at least a thousand years ahead of their time.

It is believed that their civilization rose around 2150 B.C., only about 250 years after the dispersion at Babel. Like many civilizations coming out of Babel, they had a writing system and sophisticated code of laws [1,2] By 1900 B.C. the Minoans were the powerhouse of the Mediterranean Sea and among the most formidable civilizations in the world.[3]

The Minoan Palace of Knossos was the first discovery of an advanced ancient civilization in Europe. Built around 1900 B.C., its level of advancement was equal to that of the Romans 1,400 to 2,000 years later! The palace stood four stories high and had 1,300 rooms; it is one of the most impressive buildings in the ancient world, covering an area of 479,160 feet![4]

NASA Image: Island of Crete

Libation vase (rhyton) of rock crystal with gilded ivory discs on the neck ring

Gold ibex sculpture about 10 cm long from an excavation on Santorini

Examples of the everyday beauty of items from the Minoan civilization. The libation vase above is from Zakros, another Minoan city that had a huge palace dominating the town. The ibex sculpture and the gold ring show the wealth and artistry of Minoan craftsmen. Other examples of Minoan craftsmanship and influence have been found throughout the area, including Egypt and Canaan.

1   "Destruction of the Minoan Civilization," www.explorecrete.com. http://www.explorecrete.com/archaeology/minoan-civilization-destruction.html, accessed April 9, 2013.
2   Lee Krystek, "The UnMuseum — The Lost Continent of Atlantis," www.unmuseum.org, http://www.unmuseum.org/atlantis.htm, accessed April 9, 2013.
3   History Channel, TV documentary, "Lost Worlds, Season 1, Episode 2: Atlantis," July 17, 2006.
4   Judy Powell, "Layers of Mystery — Archaeologists Look to the Earth for Minoan Fate," www.redicecreations.com, http://www.redicecreations.com/article.php?id=2127, accessed April 9, 2013.

A wooden replica of the Palace of Knossos in the Heraklion Archaeological Museum; with 1,300 rooms in the palace, it was essentially a small community, with grain mills, oil and wine presses, a theater, and very large storerooms. It also had three water systems: supply water, drainage of runoff, and waste water drainage.

The incredible Palace of Knossos had several technological advancements.

It had an extensive water supply and drainage system throughout the structure.[5] The Minoans used terracotta pipes to deliver water to the palace as well as a subterranean drainage system that ran beneath the palace to prevent flooding and to dispose of water and sewage.[6]

Their central staircase provided light to the inner rooms, by acting as a light well.

For better airflow, they used a system known as "pier-and-door partitioning." They built rows of pillars holding wooden shutters that could be opened and closed to move air within the inner rooms.[7]

5   History Channel, "Lost Worlds, Season 1, Episode 2: Atlantis."
6   Ibid.
7   Ibid.

DISCOVERIES ON THERA

Years after the discovery of the Palace of Knossos, archaeologists discovered evidence that the Minoan civilization was not limited to the island of Crete. The town of Akrotiri was found on the island of Thera in 1966. It also housed many astounding technological achievements. The town of Akrotiri displayed advanced engineering and multi-story buildings; it was also well organized, making it one of the earliest organized towns ever discovered.[8]

The citizens of Akrotiri could run fresh water into every building, and also had a sewage system throughout the entire town connecting to bathrooms within the buildings, even connecting to the second floors. The toilets of the town had an ingenious design; the waste would fall down a clay pipe to the subterranean sewage system where water from the town's drains flushed it into a cesspit. The pipes were designed in such a way that a siphon effect drew the smells down the pipes away from the lavatory. This type of system was at least a thousand years ahead of its time![9]

ON TOP OF A MOUNTAIN

Another discovery, found in the summer of 1982, has provided even more information on the Minoan civilization. The ruins of another large palace on Crete were found in Zominthos, on Mount Psiloritis (3,894 feet above sea level). The large palace covers an area of 17,000 square feet, and had at least two or three floors and 45 rooms. The ruins also include ceramic water conduits, which were most likely used as a central drainage system.[10]

Zominthos is the only Minoan building complex discovered at a high elevation. It was built strategically in order to control the surrounding area and was able to withstand the harsher elements. Many other Minoan sites have been found, each confirming and adding to the history of this great civilization. Yet with all its magnificence, this civilization did not last.

MINOANS IN AMERICA?

Some people theorize that the Minoans made it to the Americas in ancient times. They were among the greatest traders of their time and are well known for their seafaring ability. It is possible they were able to navigate the Atlantic Ocean with their technology and seamanship.

Though there is little evidence, some speculate that the Minoans not only made it to America, they actually mined copper from Michigan, around Lake Superior. There are many ancient copper mines in the area but very little copper found amongst

the natives, so some theorize that foreigners took it. The Minoans used a lot of copper and also traded a great deal to the Egyptians; some researchers believe that their mines on Cyprus were inefficient to supply the massive amounts that existed.

Some statues and a tablet with Cypriot Minoan syllabary was found in Michigan. The Native Algonquians also have genetic ties to some Eastern Mediterranean peoples providing further support that they may have had at least some interaction.

8   Ibid.
9   Ibid.
10 "Excavation History — Interactive Dig Crete – Zominthos Project," http://interactive. archaeology.org. http://interactive.archaeology.org/zominthos/introduction/ excavations/, accessed April 9, 2013.

The Demise of the Minoan Civilization

The cataclysmic volcanoes, tsunamis, and earthquakes that led to the downfall of the Minoan civilization sound like something out of a myth. However, in the past 10 to 15 years an abundance of evidence has been discovered that has solved some of the mystery surrounding this amazing civilization and its fascinating downfall.

The decline of Minoan civilization allowed the Mycenaean influence throughout the region. This fresco depicts a Mycenaean woman with a bracelet. It was found on the acropolis of Mycenae.

Catastrophic Explosion

The Minoans began a rapid demise around 1600 B.C. when the island of Thera (70 miles north of Crete) experienced one of the greatest volcanic calamities in history.[11] The center of the island of Thera is a volcano, which catastrophically erupted and destroyed the entire island. Geological records show that the volcano may have been four to ten times as powerful as the Krakatoa explosion in A.D. 1883, which is the largest in recorded history. The Krakatoa volcano extruded six cubic miles of material, and killed 36,000 people, and yet that would have been dwarfed by the massive eruption of Thera.[12] The ash from Thera's explosion has been found in the Nile delta and the Black Sea; the sound would have been heard and seen as far away as Egypt and Mesopotamia.[13]

A Mycenaean stirrup vase imported to ancient Ugarit

Disastrous Effects

The eruption not only buried the city of Akrotiri in pumice (volcanic rock), but also triggered huge tsunamis that destroyed most of the coastal residences built on Crete.[14] According to Dr. Sinolakis (a tsunami expert), up to 12 tsunamis, each around 50 feet in height, hit the shores of Crete every 30 minutes after the explosion.[15]

On the northeast tip of Crete, at a site named Palakaistro, a huge gravel deposit was found that could only have been laid down by a catastrophic tsunami. Archaeologists also discovered a building, found a quarter of a mile away from the sea, with its sea-facing wall torn off.

The greatest evidence of destruction was found on a cliff overlooking the sea. There is a layer of ash, broken pottery, cattle bones, seashells, animal teeth, and rocks that appear to have been blasted apart, then cemented back together in a massive water event. There is also another layer, which appears to be debris from a tsunami, found 90 feet above sea level![16] This type of destruction would have completely wiped out the Minoan ports, as well as their fleet.

11 Powell, "Layers of Mystery — Archaeologists Look to the Earth for Minoan Fate."
12 History Channel, "Lost Worlds, Season 1, Episode 2: Atlantis."
13 Ibid.
14 Ibid.
15 "Destruction of the Minoan Civilization," www.explorecrete.com.http://www.explorecrete.com/archaeology/minoan-civilization-destruction.html, accessed April 30, 2013.
16 Powell, "Layers of Mystery — Archaeologists Look to the Earth for Minoan Fate."

RESULT OF THE ERUPTION

Despite the massive amounts of destruction, there is evidence that the Minoans remained in Crete for another 150–200 years after the eruption. The Palace of Knossos and many other Minoan holdings were too far inland to have been affected by the tsunamis,[17] but there is evidence that massive earthquakes resulting from the volcano would have shaken the entire island of Crete, causing many of the inland dwellings to be damaged.

FINAL DOWNFALL

The great power of the Mediterranean had been devastated. They had lost their fleet as well as their ports, leaving the island nation in dire straits and incredibly vulnerable to invasion.

Around 1450 B.C. it is believed that the Mycenaeans, a rising Greek power, invaded the island of Crete. Many of the temples and buildings found on Crete show evidence of being ravaged by enemies, and there are burials from that period with bodies and weapons of the Mycenaean people. Evidence suggests that the Minoans resisted but were eventually overpowered and most of the palaces were destroyed.[18] This marked the end of the Minoan civilization.

REJECTION OF THE CREATOR

The Minoans are among the most advanced ancient civilizations ever discovered, yet they also experienced one of the most cataclysmic collapses in history. Could there be a reason they experienced such a destructive demise?

WHY DID THEY FALL?

The Bible contains many examples of great and powerful civilizations coming to their end for various reasons. We know that God is sovereign and in complete control, and Scripture clearly records that God is involved in the affairs of the nations.

When you study the rise and fall of nations throughout biblical history, there is one clear reason for the fall of these civilizations: rebellion against God caused judgment. Nations were destroyed because of their great depravity and complete rejection of God, especially in response to warning (Jeremiah 18:7–10). God is a sovereign ruler who acts as He pleases for His ultimate glory. He uses nations to do His will and to execute justice, and none are exempt. Moreover, none of us can claim righteousness. "All of us like sheep have gone astray, each of us has turned to his own way" (Isaiah 53:6).

There are many other examples; however, these are some of the most severe cases of rebellion and resulting destruction.

The area once known as Thera is now known as Santorini, and this NASA image shows how the catastrophic eruption of the volcano that was at the center of Thera devastated the island. The dark areas in the left portion of the image show the various lava flows that occurred in the 1,400 years following this deadly event.

---

17 History Channel, "Lost Worlds, Season 1, Episode 2: Atlantis."
18 "Destruction of the Minoan Civilization."

God's Sovereignty Rules Over All

"All the ends of the earth will remember and turn to the LORD, and all the families of the nations will worship before You. For the kingdom is the LORD's and He rules over the nations" (Psalm 22:27–28).

"It is He who changes the times and the epochs; He removes kings and establishes kings" (Daniel 2:21).

"And He made from one man every nation of mankind to live on all the face of the earth, having determined their appointed times and the boundaries of their habitation" (Acts 17:26).

The Nations are in Rebellion Against God

"Why are the nations in an uproar and the peoples divising a vain thing? The kings of the earth take their stand and the rulers take counsel together against the LORD and against His Anointed, saying, "Let us tear their fetters apart and cast away their cords from us!" (Psalm 2:1–3).

Nation	Pre-Flood	Babel	Sodom & Gomorrah	Tyre (Phoenicia)	
Rebellion	Mankind was exceedingly wicked and violence filled the earth (Gen. 6:5)	The people rejected God's command to scatter and instead set up their own kingdom against God. (Gen. 11:4)	The men of Sodom and Gomorrah were exceedingly wicked sinners against the Lord. (Gen. 13:13)	The leader of Tyre lifted up his heart and claimed to be a god. (Ezek. 28:1–2)	
Judgment	God brought the worldwide Flood and destroyed every living thing that walked on the earth. (Gen. 6:17)	God confused the languages of the people and scattered them over the earth. (Gen. 11:7)	The Lord rained fire and brimstone down upon the cities and utterly destroyed them. (Gen. 19:24)	God brought another nation against Tyre to destroy them with the sword. (Ezek. 28:6–10)	
Purpose	God had cleansed the earth and established a new covenant with Noah and all flesh (Gen. 9:9)	God told man to fill the earth. (Gen. 11:8)	These cities became a lasting example to those who live ungodly lives. (2 Pet. 2:6)	God was exposing the false beauty and honor of the earth. (Isa. 23:8–9)	

Moab	Egypt	Assyria	Babylon	Israel
Moab had become excessively prideful, arrogant and self-exulting. (Jer. 48:29, Isa. 16:6)	When God commanded Pharaoh to let the people go, he refused to acknowledge God and repeatedly defied God. (Ex. 5:2, 7:13)	Assyria was a nation of extreme violence. (Isa. 10:13) It was extremely prideful and haughty. (Ezek. 31:10)	Babylon destroyed and captured Judah. (2 Kings 25) The king of Babylon raised himself up above God. (Isa. 14:13–14)	Israel pursued other gods. They were violent, profaned God's Sabbath, were sexually immoral, and perverted justice. (Jer. 3:6, Ezek. 22:6–13)
God utterly devastated Moab, the people and the land. (Isa. 15)	God judged Egypt and proved His supremacy over their idols by sending the ten plagues. (Exod. 7–11)	According to the Lord's plan and purpose, He sent Babylon to destroy Assyria. (Isa. 14:24–27)	God used the Medo-Persians to utterly destroy Babylon. (Isa. 13:18–20)	God abandoned Israel and gave them over to their enemies to be scattered. (2 Kings 21:12–15)
God judged Moab in order that they would know that He was God. (Ezek. 25:11)	God displayed His signs and wonders to show His glory to both the Israelites and the Egyptians (Exod. 7:3, 5)	God executed His justice upon Assyria for their violence against Israel. (Isa. 10:12–16)	God repaid Babylon for the evil they had done against His people. (Jer. 51:24, 56)	God was calling His people back to repentance that they might serve and obey Him. (Neh. 1:4–11)

Do the Minoans Match Up?

Do we see evidence of the Babel-inspired, anti-God rebellion in the ancient Minoan civilization? After 250 years, was this nation still influenced by their goals and purposes at the Tower?

Though we don't know much, evidence (primarily their art) suggests the Minoans had a very naturalistic approach to religion, believing that nature, specifically "Mother Earth," was the supreme goddess.[19] Many of their deities were women, and their goddesses were portrayed in a very sensual way, particularly the snake goddess. Similarly, perhaps in consequence to this very sexual religion, the Minoan women were habitually immodestly attired and usually topless.

This leads us to believe the Minoan culture probably struggled with sexual immorality like many ancient cultures. Of course, in the eyes of secular historians there is little to no problem with an overly sensual culture. Today the glorification of the human body is seen in pornography, movies, fashion, etc. In the past it was exactly the same; the conduits are only slightly different.

It is also possible that the Minoans practiced human sacrifice. Some regard the evidence as inconclusive, but three different sites show indications that this morbid ritual took place.[20]

It is important to remember that there are only two religions in this world, as we state in *Genius*: "One instigated by the true God, infinite, omnipotent Creator of the universe, and leads to eternal life. The other was started by a counterfeit god in opposition to the truth, and ultimately results in death."[21]

There is no neutral ground; one is either for God or against Him, and the Minoans were most certainly not for Him. Evidence of their pagan naturalistic religion and immoral culture attests to that.[22]

The moral state of a civilization has an effect on It's survival: "Righteousness exalts a nation, but sin condemns any people" (Proverbs 14:34; NIV). God is involved in the affairs of man. He controls the rise and fall of nations. Nothing escapes His notice. The Minoans could not escape judgment if they were in continuous rebellion against the true God.

Closeup of a fresco at the Palace of Knossos

19 "Minoan Art," www.ancient-greece.org. http://www.ancient-greece.org/art/minoan-art.html, accessed May 7, 2013.
20 Leonard, John. "Palatial Remains Discovered at Ancient Kydonia, Archaeological Work in Hania, Crete, Sheds Light on Destruction of Late Bronge Age City By John Leonard | Kathimerini." Palatial Remains Discovered at Ancient Kydonia. Accessed May 20, 2015.
21 Genius: Landis, Don. *The Genius of Ancient Man.* Master Books, (Green Forest: 2012). Page 31

22 Barry P.C. Molloy, "Martial Minoans: War as Social Process, Practice and Event in Bronze Age Crete," *The Annual of the British School at Athens*, 2012, 107, p. 87–142.

ARTISTIC GENIUS

As with the Minoans, art gives us unique insight into people's religion and lifestyle. Much of the art from ancient cultures had naturalistic tendencies, including cultures that built great cities like the Minoans, as well as those who lived in more temporary homes such as caves. Following are some artistic examples of man's worship of nature.

Art — Lascaux (France)

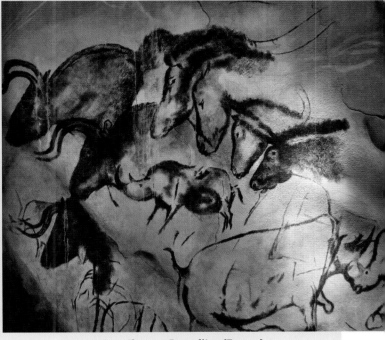

Art — Cave Chauvet-Pont-d'Arc (France)

This breath-taking complex of caves is located in southern France and is known primarily for the size, quality, and excellence of the almost 2,000 painted figures throughout.

Though there are paintings of horses, stags, bison, and even a bear and a rhino, the stars of Lascaux are the bulls. Four huge black bulls appear to run across the stone walls. One measures 17 feet long, the largest animal cave painting ever found! They likely represent an extinct species of wild cattle called Aurochs. Aurochs were massive and reportedly bad-tempered. They may be the basis for the Minoan legends of the Minotaur and were apparently used in the Minoan bull-leaping games.

This is another artistic marvel local to southern France. Like Lascaux, this cave is known for its exceptional quality. It sets itself apart for its rare exhibition of predators and the artistic finesse throughout the cave.

Thirteen different animal species, including horses, cattle, reindeer, bison, woolly rhinos, and owls, are represented as well as predators like cave bears, panthers, hyenas, and a whole wall of lions painted in blue. No human figures have been discovered in this cave.

Many caves in France feature something unique in the cave-art world and it's found in both Chauvet and Lascaux: animation. Some animals appear to have been painted with multiple heads or several extra legs. But when explorers turned off their flashlights and brought a torch down into the dark, the flickering shadows made the animals appear to move!

La Bastida [2100–2000 B.C.]

Europe's Most Formidable City

The ancient technological advancement of the Minoans is unrivaled by all other civilizations of their time except the recently discovered fortress of La Bastida. At roughly 4,000 years old by secular dating, it is among the oldest cities found on mainland Europe.[23]

La Bastida is located in the sierras of Totana, in the southeastern Murcia region of Spain.[24] It was built to protect the city on top of the hill above. The fortress had extensive walls with six towers, the perimeter stretching 1,000 feet, and the entire complex was around 13,000 square feet. Several large buildings have been found as well as a pool that could hold up to 100,000 gallons of water.[25] The most significant discovery at the site is an arched postern (back or side) gate, the oldest man-made arch in the world.[26]

La Bastida in Spain, shows remarkable evidence of fortifications and preparation (next page) for potential attacks.

Built for War

La Bastida is now labeled as Europe's most formidable city. The fortifications built there are among the most impressive ever found in Europe, and, aside from the Minoans, they are the only ancient civilization in Europe to possess such intimidating structures.[27]

The walls of the fortress stood 20 feet high and were almost 10 feet thick. Six towers have been uncovered thus far, each with a pyramid-like angled base and standing over 20 feet high.[28] Such heavy militaristic fortifications have never been found in ancient Europe, even among the Minoans!

The fortress was clearly built with warfare in mind, further exhibited by its entrance. The front gate led into a courtyard where there was another gate, guarded by a large wooden door and powerful walls. This would create a trap: even if the enemy broke through the first gate, they would have to break through the second gate while being fired upon from men in the towers surrounding the courtyard.[29] The towers and walls were built with strong lime mortar, holding the walls so tightly together that they were impermeable and so sheer that there was no way for attackers to climb them.

The most significant discovery at the site is that La Bastida was also built with a postern gate, which was a hidden arched doorway that allowed troops to flank the invading enemy. This gate may have been used to close the front gate once the enemies made it into the courtyard, trapping them between two gates.[30] The fact that the gate is an arch is even more significant. Until the discovery of the arch in La Bastida, the oldest man-made arch in the world was located in Ashkelon, Israel. This arch was supposedly built around 1850 B.C. by the Canaanite

23 Universitat Autònoma de Barcelona, "La Bastida Unearths 4,200-year-old Fortification, Unique in Continental Europe," *ScienceDaily*, Sept. 27, 2012.

24 Rossella Lorenzi, "Ancient Fortress Found in Spain," news.discovery.com. http://news.discovery.com/history/archaeology/ancient-fort-spain-121002.htm, accessed March 19, 2013.

25 Brett Smith, "La Bastida Unearthed: A 4,200 Year-Old Fort in Europe," http://www.redorbit.com/news/science/1112703239/la-bastida-fort-europe-092912/, accessed March 19, 2013.

26 Universitat Autònoma de Barcelona, "La Bastida Unearths 4,200-year-old Fortification, Unique in Continental Europe."

27 Murcia Today, "History Rewritten, 4200 Year – Old Bronze Age Fortress Unveiled At La Bastida, Totana," http://www.murciatoday.com/history-rewritten-4200-year-old-bronze-

age-fortress-unveiled-at-la-bastida-totana_13379-a.html, accessed March 19, 2013.

28 Lorenzi, "Ancient Fortress Found in Spain."

29 Murcia Today, "History Rewritten."

30 Ibid; Universitat Autònoma de Barcelona, "La Bastida Unearths 4,200-year-old Fortification, Unique in Continental Europe," http://www.itec-sde.net/en/articles/la-bastida-unearths-4-200-year-old-fortification-unique-in-continental-europe.

civilization.[31] While other civilizations would later employ the arch, it was typically only for drains and other underground structures. It wasn't until the time of Rome that arches were widely used above ground. However, the arch at La Bastida was built above ground 1,700 years before the Romans existed.[32]

MIDDLE EASTERN INFLUENCES

The fortress was built on a steep hill, clearly for strategic purposes, as it is an easily defendable position. It would have been practically impregnable. The techniques used in its construction were not seen elsewhere in Europe for another 400 years.[33]

Interestingly, its structure and location exhibit similarities to fortresses built in the Middle East and Turkey (e.g., the Hittites, Assyrians, and Philistines). Due to this connection, archaeologists have theorized that the people who built La Bastida most likely came from that area. Of course, we know that this is true — these engineers originally came from

Babel after the dispersion, taking their knowledge and skills with them as they went.

WARFARE BEFORE ITS TIME

Many people have been in shock that a civilization in Europe as old as La Bastida had fortifications designed for warfare. Most think that at that time the people in Europe were not military-minded like their eastern neighbors.

Ancient man was strategically minded, intelligent, and were waging war with one another very soon after the dispersion. The architecture of the La Bastida fortress clearly denotes a highly advanced civilization that was large enough to devote the considerable number of workers required to build the structure in such a difficult location.[34]

It seems strange that the unity mankind demonstrated at Babel was not able to last. However, it should not surprise us that the differing languages, new cultures, and man's natural tendency to desire power and control over others, particularly those he deems "different" than himself, quickly led to war.

31 Ethan Bensinger, "Ashkelon National Park: Home to the World's Oldest Arch and Nike the Winged Goddess of Victory," http://sightseeinginisrael.com/ashkelon-national-park-oldest-arch-nike, accessed March 19, 2013.
32 Linda Legner and Leslie Banker, "All About Arches," Realtor Magazine, http://realtormag.realtor.org/home-and-design/architecture-coach/article/2005/10/all-about-arches, accessed March 19, 2013.
33 Murcia Today, "History Rewritten."
34 Murcia Today, "The Agarics In Murcia," http://murciatoday.com/the-argarics-in-murcia_13377-a.html#.VGuH14fq1i0.

chapter 5

LAW AND ORDER

HARAPPAN CIVILIZATION
[2150–1900 B.C.]

As the Sumerians and Akkadians were settling in and conquering the Mesopotamian area and the Minoans were establishing their control of the Mediterranean, in India, the Harappan civilization was growing as well. Though very few people have heard of it, this ancient civilization was one of the largest during that time. It began around 2150 B.C. and fell sometime between 1900 and 1800 B.C.

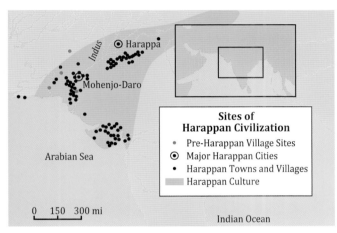

The Harappans were primarily an agricultural and mercantile community, focusing on farming and trade.[1] They had several aspects that set them apart from the other civilizations of their day such as the following:

- ▷ organized architecture
- ▷ surprising unity
- ▷ no apparent religion
- ▷ relative peace.

They also had a precise measuring system as well as a written language. Several of their cities housed up to 80,000 people at the height of their civilization, the largest being Harappa (after which the civilization was named).[2]

ORGANIZED ARCHITECTURE

The architecture of the Harappan civilization was uniquely organized and portrays a civilization run with efficiency and careful control. The large cities were designed in an extremely uniform and organized manner. It appears that the engineers planned the city before they built it, resulting in much more organization than is typically seen in ancient cities.

Mohenjo-Daro

Their structures were also uniform; they used bricks of the same material and shape for all of their structures in both Harappa and Mehenjo-Daro (the second largest city).[3] This consistent engineering is very impressive, demonstrating that the people were unified and working according to direct instructions.

UNIFIED GOVERNMENT

The Harappan civilization had a seemingly unified government and surprising lack of social classes. Typical societies of that time would have sections where the "common" people lived, then there would be the middle class area, and thirdly, a "palace" district where the nobles and/or ruler would live. The Harappan cities exhibit none of these characteristics, which has caused historians to believe that they did not have such a system of class differences.

1   Ann Musser, Emily Swanson, and David W. Koeller, "Harappan Civilization: ca. 3000–1500 B.C.," http://www.thenagain.info/webchron/india/harappa.html, accessed July 10, 2013.
2   Traci Watson, "New Views of Ancient Culture Suggest Brutal Violence," http://news.nationalgeographic.com/news/2013/13/130425-indus-civilization-discoveries-harappa-archaeology-science/.
3   Musser, Swanson, and Koeller, "Harappan Civilization: ca. 3000–1500 B.C."

One example of a board game played in the Indus Valley displayed at the Harappa Museum in Pakistan.

Their governing body is also a mystery. Did a religious priesthood run the government? A king? A council? Or was it another form of government? These questions remain unanswered due to the lack of both palaces and temples.[4]

Even though we do not know who held power, it is apparent that the government was unified, or at the very least, the people were. It is one thing to have a single well-organized city in an empire, it is an entirely different matter when all of the cities have similar layouts, all organized, built with the same material, and the same sized bricks.

The Harappans were also an extraordinarily peaceful people with small amounts of civil strife. It was once thought that they were entirely peaceful; however, recent evidence shows they were not beyond violence. Skeletons have been found evidencing that people were killed by blunt force trauma and other deaths showing there was still some conflict and crime.[5] They also had fortified cities and weapons to defend against invasion, so they were not as peaceful as originally thought.

NONEXISTENT RELIGION?

Yet another interesting characteristic of the Harappans is the absence of a central religion. If they had one, it is completely unknown and there are no temples to shed any light on the matter. They also did not seem to place any significance on burial chambers, which were simple and small.[6] Both of these aspects are almost unheard of in ancient civilizations! Is it possible that these characteristics are hints that this was a God-fearing civilization?

RAPID DOWNFALL

It has been suggested that the Harappan civilization was eventually severely weakened due to climate change (likely caused by the recession of the Ice Age). The area was quite fertile when they first settled it, however, around 2000–1900 B.C. a major shift in the climate made it quite desert-like. This weakened them, making them vulnerable to attack. It also may have made many of the Harappan people move to other locations for better farmland.[7]

Around 1900–1800 B.C. the relatively peaceful Harappans were invaded by a group known as the "Aryans." It is widely believed that these were pantheistic Indo-Europeans, a very warlike people, skilled in chariot use as well as mathematics and astronomy. They swept through the Indus Valley area and eventually controlled most of modern-day India.[8]

MYSTERIOUS UNITY

The Harappans' apparent success in peaceful unity is remarkable. The lack of evidence for religion and social caste is unheard of in ancient cultures. The cooperation, unified building materials, and planned structures are unique. Many aspects of this civilization baffle us and set it apart from other cultures. Were the Harappan citizens part of the rebellion at Babel or were they among the God-fearers? Perhaps more about them will be discovered in coming years and these mysteries will be revealed.

4   Ibid.
5   Watson, "New Views of Ancient Culture Suggest Brutal Violence."
6   Musser, Swanson, and Koeller, "Harappan Civilization: ca. 3000–1500 B.C."
7   (Maugh II)
8   Library of Congress Country Studies, "Harappan Culture," http://ancienthistory.about.com/od/indusvalleyciv/a/harappanculture.htm, accessed July 10, 2013.

BABYLON
[2100–1700 B.C.]

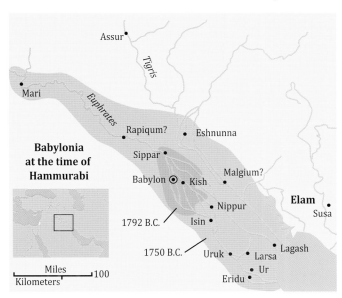

Babylonia at the time of Hammurabi

Assur · Tigris · Mari · Euphrates · Rapiqum? · Eshnunna · Sippar · Babylon ⊙ · Kish · Malgium? · 1792 B.C. · Isin · Nippur · Elam · Susa · 1750 B.C. · Uruk · Larsa · Lagash · Ur · Eridu

Miles 100
Kilometers

Back in Mesopotamia, empires began to change around 2100 B.C. At this time, the great Akkadian Empire split in half upon its downfall. The northern kingdom became Assyria and the Babylonian civilization arose in the south. The famous King Hammurabi led the Babylonians into greatness during his reign from 1792 to 1750 B.C.[9]

THE ESTABLISHMENT OF LAW

Though Hammurabi excelled as a ruler in many ways, he is primarily known as an ancient law-giver. Hammurabi's set of laws closely resembles the Mosaic Law given to Moses at Mt. Sinai. Hammurabi's Code had 282 laws and was written in Akkadian, the language of the Babylonians, allowing any citizen to read them. This was one of the first written law codes in the world.[10]

But it is important to note that Hammurabi was, by no means, the first or only king to create a law code. The Hittites, the kingdom of Ur, the kingdom of Eshnunna, as well as the Minoans all had law codes to govern their societies. In fact, the similarity of these law

codes is incredible and their resemblance to the Mosaic Law has caused many historians attempt to undermine the authority of Scripture by claiming that Moses copied men like Hammurabi when he wrote the Law. However we know that God gave Moses the Law directly.

But how did all of these early civilizations have law codes that were similar to the law Moses received much later than theirs?

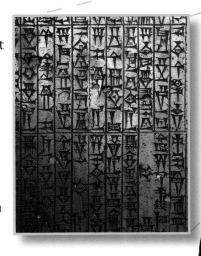

Hammurabi's Code consisted of 282 laws and was written in a language all could read and understand on this stele on display in the Louvre in France. The image at the top of the stele is showing Shamash, the god of justice, handing Hammurabi authority. It contains an early example of presumed innocence for the accused, as well as both sides being allowed to present evidence.

9   "Hammurabi." History.com. 2009. Accessed May 6, 2015.
10 Mark, Joshua J. "Hammurabi." Ancient History Encyclopedia. November 12, 2011. Accessed May 6, 2015. http://www.ancient.eu/hammurabi/.

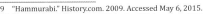

The Supremacy of God's Revelation

Remember that God has revealed truth to His people from the time of Adam and Eve. He gave them instructions, commandments, and precepts that were then passed down among the people. Hammurabi and others were likely drawing from tradition and legend when writing their laws. Even though the code of Hammurabi has many similarities to the Mosaic Law, the Mosaic Law is much more extensive and complete than any law given before it. This should be expected, because man's law will always be incomplete and faulty when compared to God's perfect revelatory law.

Another possibility for why these people had law codes is that God created mankind with a conscience; they recognized the differences between right and wrong.

> For when Gentiles who do not have the Law do instinctively the things of the Law, these, not having the Law, are a law to themselves, in that they show the work of the Law written in their hearts, their conscience bearing witness and their thoughts alternately accusing or else defending them (Romans 2:14–15).

God wrote the principles of right and wrong on their hearts. Some leaders discerned that creating a code of law based on conscience would help their societies to flourish and remain governable.

This bust was once thought to depict Hammurabi's image and was called "Head of Hammurabi." It is now believed to have predated the famous king by several hundred years.

A Great Ruler

Hammurabi is among the greatest rulers of the ancient world. During his time the Babylonian cities grew to be the largest in the world.[11] He also expanded his empire, conquering the entire Mesopotamian area within a few years. The Babylonian Empire also boasted one of the most literate populations in the Middle East.

Hammurabi was a shrewd leader and knew how to make his people follow his code of law. He used religion to maintain order and control over his kingdom, claiming that he was a messenger of the gods, sent to give the people the law. He apparently possessed special knowledge of law from the gods themselves; thus, if anyone dared oppose him they were actually opposing the gods. This allowed him to maintain order and power throughout his empire.

It is possible that Hammurabi got this idea from Babylonian mythology. In Babylon during his time, Marduk was the chief god. According to myth, Marduk rose above all gods during a war. After defeating the goddess Taimat, Marduk claimed the mythical "Tablet of Destinies" for himself; supposedly whoever possessed this tablet would rule the universe. There are many tales like this in which a certain item, or knowledge, provides power.

People have a natural tendency to believe in something greater than themselves. This comes directly from our knowledge of the one true God. Remember, all mankind knows that God exists for He has made it apparent in all of creation ("*because that which is known about God is evident within them; for God made it evident to them.*" Romans 1:19; NASB). When people reject God as the great authority, they open themselves up to be dominated by any other power. Rulers can use this natural intuition of a greater authority against their people in order to rule with fear, supremacy, and complete control.

11 ibid

DERINKUYU (TURKEY)

[SOMETIME BETWEEN 1500–1000 B.C.]

It's not every day you hear about entire cities built thousands of years ago boasting sophisticated architecture, design, and careful organization — underground! Derinkuyu, a massive subterranean city that could have housed up to 20,000 people, is literally a mine for unearthing evidence of ancient genius.

Derinkuyu is a huge, 18-story complex with meeting rooms, halls, wells, ventilation shafts, wine and oil presses, tunnels, and stables that descend deep into the earth. It was incredibly defensible with narrow tunnels and huge stones to block entrances. Natural wells inside provided clean drinking water, and ventilation shafts kept the air fresh and temperatures even. Able to house thousands of people as well as provisions and even livestock, Derinkuyu was a veritable fortress and a refuge for a time of war.

The tunnels and rooms of the large, multi-level city of Derinkuyu found in Cappadocia, Turkey are underground. It is just one of hundreds of underground cities that have been found in that part of the world. The ancient Greek historian Xenophon wrote of people in this region of Anatolia living underground in his work *Anabasis.*

Egyptians

[2100–1200 b.c. Peak 1600–1200 b.c.]

As Babylon rose out of the ashes of Akkad, Egypt also began to rise in power and distinction. The Egyptian civilization was one of the greatest powers to exist in the ancient world and is responsible for some of the most imposing structures ever built.

Though Egypt was a prominent nation for many years, it rose to greatness under the leadership of Thutmose III (ruled from 1479 to 1426 B.C.),[12] and became the dominant world power. The Egyptians remained powerful for several hundred years, up to their last great pharaoh Ramses II, also known as Ramses the Great.

Kings as Gods

The Egyptian civilization was among the many ancient civilizations that actually lifted their rulers to god-like status. The pharaohs were viewed as descendants of the gods, giving them the right to govern and making it easy for them to maintain their rule. No revolts are mentioned in recorded Egyptian history, probably because no one wanted to openly rebel against the gods' chosen ruler. The people were bound to maintain the status quo because in the mind of an Egyptian, open rebellion against the gods' chosen ruler would result in severe punishment, even into the afterlife.

Thutmose III

Many historians would claim that Thutmose III was the greatest conqueror in the history of the Egyptian Empire. He was the heir of the only known female pharaoh, Hatshepsut. He co-reigned with his mother for 22 years (this co-rulership started when he was two), and commanded the military during the last years of this co-reign.

Upon his mother's death he started to expand the empire, creating the largest Egyptian empire to date. He conducted 17 military campaigns over 20 years, which resulted in the capture of 350 cities. His empire stretched from Syria to Nubia.

He detailed his accomplishments in the "holy of holies" at the Karnak Temple of Amun, effectively immortalizing himself as Egypt's greatest pharaoh. Though he constructed many temples, his greatest architectural achievement was his enormous obelisk, which still remains the tallest obelisk ever cut.

---

12 Peter F. Dorman, "Thutmose," *Encyclopedia Britannica*, http://www.britannica.com/EBchecked/topic/594493/Thutmose-III, accessed October 14, 2014.

ABU SIMBEL

Ramses II built Abu Simbel to honor himself. It was an incredible temple; its craftsmanship and immensity set it apart from most ancient monuments, but its purpose was the same — the glorification of man.

At its entrance, the temple has a façade depicting four colossal statues carved out of the solid stone of the mountain. The figures are 67 feet high; three of them are representations of Egypt's greatest gods (Ptah, the god of creation; Amun-Ra, the sun god; and Horus, the midday sun) and the fourth, is a statue of Ramses himself! He deified and included himself in the upper echelon of the gods.

The entrance to the temple leads to a massive man-made cave going back 185 feet, with two rows of 30-foot statues lining the hall. Inside, Ramses II had stories written down to tell of his victories over the Hittite Empire at Kadesh. The entire temple was dedicated to displaying his achievements and his honor. The innermost shrine contained four statues, which were only illuminated by the sun on February 22 and October 22 (an example of archaeoastronomy). These were likely significant dates in Ramses' life, perhaps his coronation and birth.[13]

RAMSES II

Ramses II was also an incredible conqueror, and he may have even been Egypt's greatest pharaoh. He reigned for an astonishing 66 years (from 1279 to 1213 B.C.) and is most well known for his massive building projects. His two most famous building projects were Abu Simbel and the Ramesseum.

---

13 Mark, Joshua J. "Abu Simbel." Ancient History Encyclopedia. January 6, 2013. Accessed May 11, 2015. http://www.ancient.eu/Abu_Simbel/.

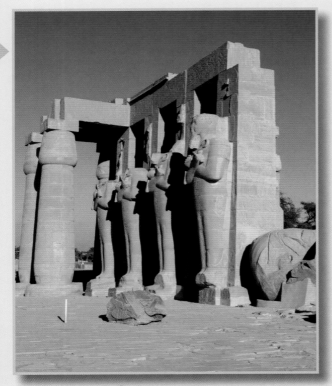

RAMESSEUM

The Ramesseum was another structure that Ramses II built to honor the god Ra, as well as himself. It is another monument that displays the extreme pride of Ramses II by placing himself among the Egyptian gods.

Like Abu Simbel, the Ramesseum is among the ancient world's greatest works. It stretches over 900 feet long by 550 feet wide. It contains a seated statue of Ramses II that stands 57 feet tall. The entire temple is filled with murals of his victories over the Hittites, claiming that he destroyed and scattered over 100,000 men and 2,500 chariots in the battle of Kadesh. It sets Ramses II up as a god among men; it is a shrine unto himself and his accomplishments, another testament to his pride.

Ramses II wanted to be known as the greatest of pharaohs. The characteristic human pride, the desire to gain glory, reverence, and honor for oneself, displays his rejection of the Almighty God.

In reality, man doesn't ever deserve glory, and we should never seek glory for ourselves. Yet we can't seem to escape from our goal to make a name for ourselves and gain more power. [14]

---

14 "Ancient Egypt - Ramesseum." Ancient Egypt - Ramesseum. Accessed May 11, 2015. http://ancient-egypt.co.uk/ramasseum/index.htm.

ANCIENT PANTHEONS

Egyptian religion was complicated; however, it was similar to almost every other religion of that time period. Like most civilizations, the Egyptians saw the sun god Ra as the greatest and most powerful of their pantheon. This was probably because the ancient people held the heavens in such high regard and the sun was the greatest light in the sky.

It is interesting that, depending on a civilization's proximity and usage of water, sometimes the sea god would be raised to higher prominence. Civilizations that spent a great deal of time seafaring knew the incredible power of the ocean and so the sea god became one of the highest in their pantheon. Some civilizations such as the Greeks and Norse held the thunder god as the supreme power.

Regardless of the choice made for a civilization's supreme god, each god had one common factor: it was considered the greatest force in nature. It is a perfect example of Romans 1:25: "*For they exchanged the truth of God for a lie, and worshiped and served the creature rather than the Creator.*"

Ancient man created gods out of the things they could see, the creatures they revered, and the forces of nature that they feared. Consider the list of pagan worship that Israel was warned about:

Abu Simbel temples — Nubia in southern Egypt. To preserve it from being submerged with the formation of Lake Nasser, the complex was relocated in 1969, saving Pharaoh Ramesses II's monument to himself and three other "gods" in addition to his family presented in smaller statues of the gods.

"... do not act corruptly and make a graven image for yourselves in the form of any figure, the likeness of **male or female**, the likeness of any **animal** that is on the earth, the likeness of any **winged bird** that flies in the sky, the likeness of **anything that creeps on the ground**, the likeness of any **fish** that is in the water below the earth. And beware not to lift up your eyes to heaven and see **the sun and the moon and the stars**, all the host of heaven, and be drawn away and worship them and serve them ..." (Deuteronomy 4:16–19, emphasis added).

The pagan nations of ancient times were eager to worship finite, limited beings, rather than the infinite Creator of the universe who holds all power. What a poor substitute such men have chosen in their rebellious ignorance.

chapter 6

Sea to Sea

Olmecs

[1500–400 B.C.]

Across the Atlantic Ocean, the dispersed people from Babel managed to travel the innumerable miles and start to develop advanced civilizations as early as 1500 B.C. One such early civilization has been called the "Mother Culture" of Mexico. Though we know next to nothing about them, the Olmec are considered one of the first civilizations to develop into greatness in the Americas. Other Mexican civilizations supposedly grew from the seeds of this ancient people. It is believed they were located mainly near the southern Gulf of Mexico but that their influence touched regions all over the country.

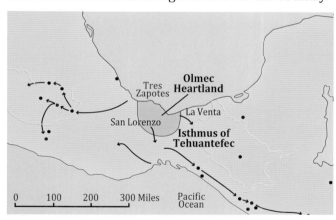

The Olmec are an interesting mystery. While we can study the relatively few ruins and works of art they left behind, the artifacts seem to be representing mere ghosts. Try as we might, we cannot decipher who these ghosts really were.

We do not know anything about the Olmecs' social structure, their ceremonies, their beliefs, what language they spoke, or what traditions they passed on. Even their real ethnicity is still debated; the humid jungles they inhabited have swallowed them up, leaving very little to trace over the centuries (the natural conditions have even erased skeletal remains). Despite the lofty views history claims concerning this "Mother Culture," not much is actually certain.

Remnants and Speculation

Researchers believe that in the early years, San Lorenzo Tenochtitlán was the center of the Olmec civilization. However, in 950 B.C., many of the monuments were destroyed or defaced, perhaps by an internal uprising of some sort. By 900 B.C. it was mostly abandoned. The city of La Venta rose in prominence soon after.

At La Venta, evidence of spectacular wealth and power have been found, including the largest Mesoamerican structure of its time, the Great Pyramid. Beneath the various mounds of the La Venta pyramid complex, more than 50 caches of buried objects have been found. The caches include polished mirrors, carefully finished serpentine blocks, and precious jade celts.[1] (Both the Olmec and the Chinese cultures were known for their reverence for jade.)

An exquisitely-carved jadeite mask; for the Olmec, the color green and symbol of corn represented rejuvenation after death.

Beyond their apparent wealth, more distressing speculations of infant sacrifice have also arisen from ritual art found at La Venta. A carving depicting a limp baby in the arms of a man, in addition to the skeletons of newborn children found at a site called El Manati, lead some to believe the Olmec practiced child sacrifice.

---

1   "La Venta," http://www.ancient-wisdom.co.uk/mexicolaventa.htm, accessed October 15, 2014.

The Famous Colossal Heads

The Olmec are probably most well known for the gigantic stone heads they carved and left behind. The first was found at Tres Zapotes in 1862:

> Cleared of the surrounding earth it presented an awe-inspiring spectacle. Despite its great size the workmanship is delicate and sure, the proportions perfect. Unique in character among aboriginal American sculptures, it is remarkable for its realistic treatment. The features are bold and amazingly Negroid in character. . . .[2]

These heads seem to indicate that the Olmec likely had a connection to Africa. It is believed they may have had the capability to sail across the Atlantic, or they had visitors who could. Interestingly, the Olmec also produced art that depicted men with beards and mustaches (something that Native Americans did not typically depict in their art."), causing researchers to believe they had interaction with civilizations from across both the Pacific and Atlantic.

Earliest known feathered serpent representation — found in the Olmec site of La Venta

An Influential Legacy

Though the Olmec supposedly ceased to exist 1,500 years before the rise of the Aztec Empire, the Aztecs have preserved haunting traditions and accounts about them.

The Olmec are credited with influencing the later civilizations of Mexico in several ways. Cities and the building style of Olmec sites such as La Venta seem to be copied by later civilizations and the Olmec used temple mounds, human sacrifice (potentially), and a religion of many gods long before the Mayans and Aztecs. The ancient calendar used in Mexico and even the ritual ball game of the Aztecs is believed to have originated with the Olmec as well.[3]

The Olmec are also credited with the first depiction of what would later become a significant symbol in American civilizations: the feathered serpent.

So even though we know very little about the specifics of this great ancient culture, the influences of their beliefs and practices echoed into the centuries that came after them. They had disappeared by 400 B.C. and nobody knows where they went or what happened to them.

One of 17 colossal Olmec heads. Each is unique and realistic, but how the stones were transported before being carved, and even who is depicted by the heads, are still mysteries to be solved. It is thought they may have been representative of rulers.

2   Matthew W. Stirling, "Discovering the New World's Oldest Dated Work of Man," *National Geographic Magazine* 76 (August 1939): p. 183–218.

3   "The Ancient Olmec Civilization," http://www.aztec-history.com/olmec-civilization.html, accessed October 6, 2014.

"Were-Jaguars"

The jaguar was an important emblem for most Meso-American cultures, probably because it was the most powerful animal in their region. It was a sacred figure that was thought to belong to another space, not of this world. Some cultures believed that kings and nobles were descended from this feline.[4]

The "were-jaguar," a half-human, half-jaguar creature, appeared in Olmec art as early as 1500 B.C.[5] Researchers believe that the were-jaguar was probably some sort of deity that was worshiped by the Olmec people. They crafted statues, masks, bas-reliefs, pottery, and figurines depicting this figure. Interestingly, many of the images are of infant were-jaguars, causing some to believe they were connected to birth defects or diseases.[6]

Others believe that the Olmec saw the jaguar as the alter ego of the shamans, an "avatar" of the living and the dead. They suggest the images represent Olmec men transforming into jaguars, and the grimacing jaguar-like facial features of the depictions convey the emotional, mental, and physical stress that was endured through the transformation — crossing the threshold between two worlds.[7]

Olmec altar-throne displayed at the archaeological park, Villahermosa, Veracruz. The central figure-ruler is sitting in a niche surmounted by a stylized jaguar snout. He also holds a rope that skirts the bottom of the monument. The scene may represent an Olmec origin myth. Mexico. Olmec. 1100–450 B.C. La Venta, Olmec site.

Phoenicians
[1600–350 B.C. Peak 1200–750 B.C.]

Not every civilization grew to power through the same means; each exhibited their genius and strength in different ways. While some were violent conquerors, others built incredible monuments, and still others invented organized systems of law.

Another method through which to gain might and wealth was through trade and seafaring. The Phoenicians were one of the most advanced seafaring civilizations to ever exist (circa 1500–500 B.C.). It is believed by some historians that they could actually sail across the Atlantic at will and perhaps around Africa as well.[8]

Greek-style sarcophagus found in northern Lebanon in the burial grounds of Antarados.

4 "The Black Jaguar: A Powerful Ancient Maya Symbol," http://www.theyucatantimes.com/2012/11/the-black-jaguar-a-powerful-ancient-maya-symbol/, accessed October 23, 2014.
5 Ibid
6 George Milton and Roberto Gonzalo, "Jaguar Cult — Down's Syndrome — Were-Jaguar," *Expedition* (online), Summer 1974, http://www.penn.museum/documents/publications/expedition/PDFs/16-4/Gonzalo.pdf, accessed October 23, 2014.

7 "The Olmec Gods," http://www.aaanativearts.com/ancient-indians/olmec-gods.htm, accessed October 23, 2014.
8 Gore, Rick. "Who Were the Phoenicians? - National Geographic Magazine." Who Were the Phoenicians? - National Geographic Magazine. October 1, 2004. Accessed May 11, 2015. http://ngm.nationalgeographic.com/features/world/asia/lebanon/phoenicians-text/1.

INCREDIBLE NAVIGATORS

The Phoenicians were renowned for their excellent navigational skills and shipbuilding techniques. They introduced a new way to craft durable ships by using "mortise-and-tenon" joints, which provided much greater strength than the design of earlier boats in history. This stronger construction allowed them to sail much longer distances over rough water. It is therefore very possible that they made it across the Atlantic — their ships were certainly capable of doing so.[9]

There is other evidence supporting this theory as well. Jonathan Gray (a controversial author and archaeologist) claims that there are Phoenician inscriptions found in North America and Brazil. Others claim that there are linguistic similarities in the Phoenician, Samoan, and Tahitian languages.

Many claim that it may have been the Phoenicians who spread the idea that the Atlantic Ocean was not navigable, thereby protecting their trade empire with exclusive access to the Americas. While people still debate whether or not the Phoenicians made it to the New World, it is widely accepted that they at least made it past the Straits of Gibraltar.

---

9   Ibid

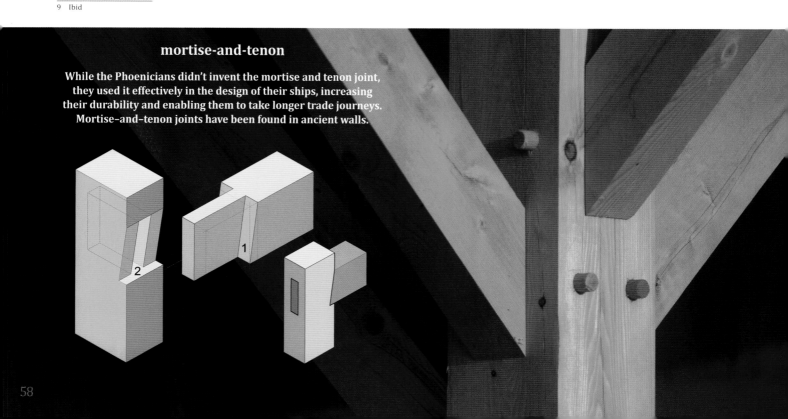

mortise-and-tenon

While the Phoenicians didn't invent the mortise and tenon joint, they used it effectively in the design of their ships, increasing their durability and enabling them to take longer trade journeys. Mortise–and–tenon joints have been found in ancient walls.

Power through Trade

While they were certainly not among the greatest military civilizations to ever exist, the Phoenicians' abilities in seafaring, engineering, and trading allowed them to gain a great deal of power and influence throughout the civilizations located on the Mediterranean Sea. They supplied goods to nations that were greater in power than they were, which made them untouchable. To destroy them would be to destroy a country's trade infrastructure.

In biblical texts, Tyre, a city in Phoenicia, is described as incredibly wealthy: "*Whose merchants were princes, whose traders were honored of the earth*" (Isaiah 23:8). The city had mighty pillars, riches, and much merchandise; it was a city of renown that was mighty on the sea (Ezekiel 23).

However, this did not save them from God's judgment. The Phoenicians were among the many civilizations that were judged by God due to their pride. God brought Nebuchadnezzar against the city of Tyre (586–573 B.C.) saying, "*I will bring you to a dreadful end, and you shall be no more*" (Ezekiel 26:21 ESV).

Cyrus the Great (from Persia) conquered the nation in 539 B.C., and the distinct Phoenician influence declined. Though they continued to build ships for the Persian navy, many Phoenicians migrated south to Carthage and others were slowly absorbed into the cultures around them. Eventually, Alexander the Great utterly destroyed Tyre and executed hundreds of its citizens in 322 B.C., causing even more people to flee to Carthage.

Obviously it does not matter how "indispensible" you think you are, God is not swayed by wealth or influence. Even though the Phoenicians thought they were untouchable, they were sadly mistaken in their pride.

Carthage

[400–150 B.C.]

Even after the fall of Tyre and collapse of the Phoenician civilization, a remnant of seafarers survived in North Africa. This remnant would become another one of the Mediterranean superpowers, Carthage. The small town on the coast grew to become the richest city on the Mediterranean.[10]

When it was first founded by the Phoenicians around 830 B.C., Carthage was simply a small port on the coast. It wasn't until the fifth century B.C. that Carthage began to establish some form of dominance in the Mediterranean.[11]

Carthage was one of the great powers around the Mediterranean for many years, rivaling the early Roman Republic. They continued in the footsteps of their Phoenician predecessors with their sea dominance. It was due to their shipwright and navigational prowess that they were able to keep up with early Rome. Their navy was the greatest in the world and it kept them in power. However, as the Romans grew stronger and the Carthaginian ships expanded their empire, eventual conflict was inevitable.

Glass pendant found in the necropolis of Carthage (modern-day Tunisia)

10 Joshua J. Mark, "Carthage," Ancient History Encyclopedia, http://www.ancient.eu/carthage/, accessed October 15, 2014.
11 Ibid.

A Most Impressive Harbor

Around the third to second century B.C., the Carthaginians constructed the most impressive docks ever built during their time. Their enormous man-made harbor had a single entrance 70 feet wide that could be blocked with a chain stretching across. Inside, there were two separate marinas, one for the merchant ships and the other for their impressive navy.

The trading harbor was built with large wharves, which allowed ships to rapidly unload their goods to the markets. The military harbor was circular. A series of 30 docks were arranged symmetrically in the center while an additional 140 docks were arranged along the perimeter. The entire military harbor could hold 220 ships. It was by far the most formidable harbor of the ancient world.

A large tower rose from within the harbor, allowing the Carthaginians to see enemy vessels approaching from miles away. The design of the docks not only provided an incredible defensive structure against enemy ships, it also allowed for rapid deployment. It benefited their navy, and also gave merchants a safe place to dock and trade goods.[12]

12 Engineering an Empire: Carthage. Directed by Cannon, Mark. Performed by Peter Weller. United States: History Channel, 11/06/2006. TV series.

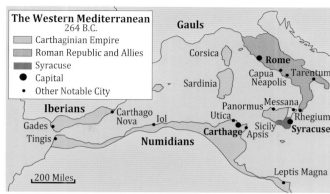

ram at the front would allow the sailors to destroy enemy ships, typically sinking a ship in one blow.

The Carthaginians mass-produced each part and utilized assembly lines to build these ships. Their design and ability to rapidly construct warships displayed their engineering prowess, though it would not be enough to save them.

The fall of Carthage was inevitable; Rome would not be challenged on their road to becoming the greatest superpower ever known. After Rome developed its own navy, it was only a matter of time. A series of several different invasions and wars from 264 through 146 B.C. ended with the destruction and burning of the great city of Carthage.[13]

With the destruction of Carthage, it seems the ability to sail past the straits of Gibraltar also ended. Travel to the Americas across the Atlantic would halt until Leif Erikson and the Vikings traveled there around A.D. 1000.

Powerful Ships

Carthage also boasted the most powerful ships of their day, unmatched until the Romans were able to reverse engineer one of Carthage's ships.

The greatest type of ship was called the Quinquereme, which was an upgraded version of the Greek Trireme. The Quinquereme had five banks of oars on each side, allowing for an incredible amount of power. The ship was built for speed, maneuverability, and effective combat. Quinqueremes were 120 feet long, 16 feet wide, and could hold up to 420 sailors. A bronze-covered

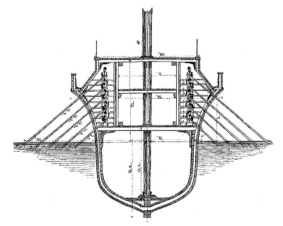

19th-century depiction of the oar system on a quinquereme

13 Ibid.

Empire of Secrets

One of the reasons cross-Atlantic travel ended after the fall of the Carthaginians was because they were very secretive about their techniques of navigation. This secrecy in the area of technology and advancement was very common in the ancient world. The higher-class citizens would maintain power through secrets of this sort. In the case of Phoenicia and Carthage, they maintained power over trade through their navigational secrets.

The phrase "knowledge is power" comes to mind when studying the various civilizations and rulers who used secret technology and knowledge to control their subjects. Where did this idea come from? Why is knowledge held so highly? Think back to the very first sin; why did Eve take from the tree and eat? Because Satan used man's thirst for knowledge, and alluded that the knowledge would make him "like God." Satan equates knowledge, specifically having all knowledge, with being God.

Likewise, many of the rulers in history maintained their power through knowledge. They dominated others because they knew more. Once Carthage lost its advantage of preeminent shipbuilding, it fell to the new rising power.

Pyramids: Testament to Similarity

Ancient seafarers, like the Phoenicians and Carthaginians, may be responsible for creating two of the most intriguing pyramid sites in the world. The mysterious pyramids, built on the islands of Tenerife and Mauritius, are not known for advanced megalithic construction or incredibly sophisticated technology; rather these two island sites are fascinating due to their geographic locations and the similarities between them.

Tenerife Pyramid

Tenerife

Mauritius

On both Tenerife and Mauritius, the pyramids:

- are built in complexes with multiple structures in one area

- are all step pyramids

- are built using identical construction techniques

- are built with mostly volcanic rock

- contain 6–11 terraces/steps

- stand no more than 12 meters in height

- are astronomically aligned (or are theorized to be).

It is, in fact, next to impossible to differentiate between the pyramids on Tenerife and those on Mauritius.[14]

These incredible similarities may not seem all that remarkable unless you also know this one last fascinating aspect: these two islands are THOUSANDS of miles apart, separated by the continent of Africa.

14 Antoine Gilgal, "Seven Pyramids Identified on the African Island of Mauritius," 2009, Gilgal Research, http://www.gigalresearch.com/uk/pyramides-maurice.php. accessed November 5, 2013.

China

[1000 B.C.–1500 A.D.
Peak around 250 B.C.–1500 A.D.]

While China was settled less than 1,000 years after Babel, it was never a truly great, united nation until Emperor Qin Shi Huangdi rose to power around 250 B.C.

The Great Tomb of Qin Shi Huangdi

In 1974, archaeologists in China discovered a large mausoleum underneath a massive ancient mound. It is believed to be the tomb of China's first emperor. Nearby, a mile east of the tomb and thought to be guarding its entrance, large pits were found with thousands of terracotta soldiers buried inside.

The great emperor's name was Ying Zheng, later changed to Qin Shi Huangdi (pronounced "chin-shuh-hwang-di").[15]

Qin Shi Huangdi

Emperor Qin Shi Huangdi was responsible for turning China into a great nation. The Chinese civilization was never united until Ying Zheng came to power in 246 B.C. at the young age of 13.[16] His father was the king of the Qin state, and when Ying Zheng succeeded him, he used ambition and the powerful military might of Qin to subjugate other nearby states. He was able to conquer his neighbors through his use of horsemen and standardized weapons. He also utilized more iron for weapons and armor, giving his army an advantage. By 221 B.C., he had unified six warring states and took the name Qin Shi Huangdi, which means "The First Emperor of China."[17]

Qin not only took control of the majority of China, he also set up a well-organized empire that would last for years to come. He standardized coins, weights, and measures, throughout China as well as a writing system. He also built roads and canals to increase the flow and rate at which trade was conducted. His network of roads stretched approximately 4,000 miles and included some roads up to 40 feet wide, complete with a lane reserved for imperial (royal) members. He is also credited with building the first version of the Great Wall.[18]

Emperor Qin Shi Huangdi's unique and beautiful terracotta army; (top left) each soldier is different, and once vividly painted, possibly modeled after real soldiers of the time.

15 "Mausoleum of Emperor Qinshihuang (259 BC- 210 BC)." Mausoleum of Emperor Qinshihuang (259 BC- 210 BC). Accessed May 11, 2015. http://www.china.org.cn/english/features/atam/115132.htm.

16 Joshua J. Mark, "Shi Huangti," *Ancient History Encyclopedia*, December 18, 2012, http://www.ancient.eu/Shi_Huangti/, accessed October 30, 2014.

17 Ibid.

18 Engineering an Empire: China. Directed by Cannon, Mark. Performed by Peter Weller. United States: History Channel, 12/11/2006. TV series.

The Great Wall of China

Qin Shi Huangdi started one of the greatest building projects in human history: a massive wall to keep enemies out and his people in.

During his day, the Great Wall was not quite as impressive as it currently is today. It started out as a mud brick wall. First, the builders would tamp the foundation to provide a solid base, and then a wooden frame was built to contain the wall as they laid down layers of gravel and sticks combined with clay. This layer would then be repeated until the desired height was achieved. Once the wooden frame was removed, all that remained was a solid wall of tamped earth and clay. While not quite as impressive as the wall we see today, it was still an incredible achievement of human engineering.

The wall also provided a rapid communication route, allowing Chinese troops on the border to keep each other informed of enemy movements. A guard tower was placed every 700 to 1,000 yards to provide additional protection. The wall extended over a distance of 3,000 miles during Qin's reign, and though it was formidable it was more symbolic than effective. It was not overly difficult to circumnavigate.

During the Han Dynasty (206 B.C.–A.D. 220) the wall was extended and fortress watchtowers were placed one to three miles apart, though they could be as close as 500 feet apart in enemy territory. The wall we see today was reinforced with stone during the Ming Dynasty, during which time the wall reached a total of 6,000 miles, making it one of the wonders of the world.[19]

Building His Tomb

Shortly after Qin Shi Huangdi came into power, he ordered the construction of his now-famous mausoleum. He never saw his masterpiece completed. According to Siam Qian (a Chinese historian), more than 700,000 workers were involved in building his tomb, but they were cut short by uprisings in 209 B.C., shortly after Qin's death in 210 B.C.

Qin Shi Huangdi's tomb is one of the greatest examples in China of both ancient man's intellect and his pride. Built like an underground city, the tomb is located beneath a man-made mound nearly the size of the Great Pyramid in Egypt. Above ground, 30-foot walls divided the site, which was split into outer city, inner city, and mausoleum complexes.

The mausoleum was a large pyramid mound that rose over the landscape nearly 400 feet. However, it is what is beneath the surface that amazes modern historians. Supposedly the underground chamber, 1,600 by 1,700 feet, equal to 580 basketball courts, was filled with incredible treasures: rivers of mercury, pavilions of gold, and pearls on the ceiling to represent the night sky. But whether or not the inside of the tomb is as magnificent as the stories say is unknown. The Chinese have refused to excavate until archaeology has reached a level capable of preserving whatever remains inside.[20]

19 Ibid.
20 Ibid.

There are believed to be even more beautifully crafted terracotta figures, waiting to be discovered.

THE TERRACOTTA ARMY

Qin Shi Huangdi ordered the construction of the incredible Terracotta Army to guard him in the afterlife. The creation of these soldiers required a massive amount of work. One pit alone contained over 6,000 horses and warriors, and another 1,300 were found in a different pit. Each soldier has unique facial features and clothing!

The clay that was used to construct the army was much harder than anything utilized before. The Chinese used blast furnaces known as kilns, which allowed them to heat the terracotta up to 2,000 degrees Fahrenheit! Each statue could weigh up to 600 pounds and ranged in height from 5'8" to 6'2", which was considerably taller than the average man in those days. The armor that is replicated on the soldiers was lacquered leather, boots with cleats, and caps that signified each soldier's rank.

Besides the soldiers, some clay figures were found modeled after acrobats, dancers, and musicians. There are believed to be around 600 pits, and only a handful have been excavated thus far.[21]

21 "Mausoleum of Emperor Qinshihuang (259 BC- 210 BC)." Mausoleum of Emperor Qinshihuang (259 BC- 210 BC). Accessed May 11, 2015.

A Greek Connection?

It is now believed that Qin Shi Huangdi may have had some Western influence when he ordered the creation of his Terracotta Army. According to recently discovered Chinese texts, ambassadors were sent west to learn about the nations in that area. (Note that by this time Alexander the Great had already swept across Persia, stretching Greek influence all the way to the Indus River. This spread of Greek culture, now known as Hellenization, drastically changed the course of human culture.) The Chinese ambassadors came back with fantastic tales of beautiful buildings, grand kings, and, most importantly, marvelous, realistic statues.

Apparently the emperor liked the Greek and Western style, and it appears that he replicated it in his commissioned statues. Shortly after these reports, the Terracotta Army was built — the first realistic sculptures that the Chinese fashioned. It is amazing to see the impact each culture can have on another. It also attests to the fact that there were connections between these different cultures even in the earliest of times of history.[22]

Search for Immortality

Qin Shi Huangdi was obsessed with finding a way to immortality, and his impressive tomb and army of statues were part of his effort to make himself comfortable and successful in the afterlife.[23] Chinese legend states that Qin Shi Huangdi discovered "The Three Islands of the Immortals," which were home to a magical herb that would give everlasting life. According to this legend, the islands would only admit "uncorrupted children," and so Qin Shi Huangdi reportedly sent several thousand children to find these mythical islands, but none returned. Four years later he sent three alchemists and only one returned to tell the emperor about a great fish that was guarding the Islands.

According to legend, the emperor himself conducted the final retrieval mission. He is said to have used a repeating crossbow to kill the great fish, but in a fatal twist of irony, instead of finding the magical healing herbs he contracted a fatal illness. He died at age 49, leaving his son to rule. His advisor took power instead, but after Qin Shi Huangdi's death the empire fell into civil war, resulting in a change in power after only four years. The short-lived Qin Dynasty was replaced by the Han Dynasty.[24]

Emperor Qin Shi Huangdi's search for immortality is strikingly similar to that of Gilgamesh, though they are not connected in any way. It simply goes to show the common human desire to live forever, again reminding us of what man lost in the Garden. As it says in Ecclesiastes, God has placed eternity into our hearts (3:11). History has proven that most men seek after eternity by their own strength and means, instead of from God.

In the 6th century, the Chinese built a gigantic canal (1,200 miles long), employing 5 million workers over 6 years.

22 Jarus, Owen. "Terracotta Warriors Inspired by Ancient Greek Art." LiveScience.com. December 10, 2013. Accessed May 11, 2015. http://m.livescience.com/41828-terracotta-warriors-inspired-by-greek-art.html.

23 Ibid.
24 Ibid.

chapter 7

St. Stephens Gate, Jerusalem

GOD'S SOVEREIGN HAND

ISRAEL

[1096–586 B.C.]

We now come to the time period in history where we begin to see God actively working specifically with His chosen people, the nation of Israel. Israel is a fascinating civilization to compare and contrast to other nations because we know so much about how exactly God was working with them. By 1400 B.C., God had brought the ancient Israelites out of Egypt and into the Promised Land of Canaan. After Joshua's successful conquest of the land, the people lived in their 12 tribes for several hundred years, somewhat united, and governed by various judges whom God equipped throughout the years. Yet they were never unified under the dominion of a single human ruler until Saul was anointed King in 1096 B.C., and the Jewish nation did not flourish (with wealth and power) until the time of King David and his son Solomon.

The golden age of Israel arose under King Solomon (1016–976 B.C.), during which time he built the magnificent temple of God in Jerusalem, as well as an incredible royal house for himself. There was nothing that could compare to these structures during their time. The wealth and splendor of Solomon and his kingdom were unrivaled — silver was not even considered valuable in his days, it was "as common as stones" (1 Kings 10:21, 27). His wisdom and provision of justice for his people was famous. "All the earth was seeking the presence of Solomon, to hear his wisdom which God had put in his heart" (1 Kings 10:24).

The dedication of the temple was perhaps the highest point in Israel's history. "Never again do we find the nation, as a whole, living in such peace and prosperity and apparently so completely devoted to the Lord. Both king and people were united in obedience to the law of God."[1] It is an important observation to make because even this nation, chosen by God and established specifically to

worship Him, only prospered when they submitted themselves to His authority.

WHAT MADE ISRAEL DIFFERENT?

One of the most distinctive characteristics of the Israelite civilization was their monotheistic beliefs and elaborate, detailed code of law. Israel recognized the one true God, unlike the nations surrounding them. They were required to worship only at the temple in Jerusalem, and their religious practices were specific and strict, according to God's direction and design.

The law that God instigated for His people was also unique. It required high standards of ethics among the people, including love and respect to all, even women and foreigners. The kings were expected to rule with fairness and justice, and to lead the people in the proper worship of God. God set Israel apart and they stood out in many ways among the pagan civilizations because God was using them to teach the world about Himself.

---

1   Paul N. Benware, *Survey of the Old Testament* (Chicago, IL: Moody Publishers, 2003), p. 126.

Jehu, king of Israel, giving tribute to King Shalmaneser III of Assyria

How Was Israel the Same?

After the glorious reign of King Solomon, the nation was divided (Israel in the north and Judah in the south) and they were weakened by civil war. This division was a judgment from God because King Solomon, in all his wisdom and prosperity, failed to keep God's Law. In Deuteronomy 17, God instructed the kings not to multiply horses (military might), wives, or silver and gold. But Solomon flagrantly violated all three of these commands! Just like the pagan kings around him, Solomon rejected God's commands.

> For when Solomon was old, his wives turned his heart away after other gods.
> . . . For Solomon went after Ashtoreth the goddess of the Sidonians and after Milcom the detestable idol of the Ammonites.
> . . . Then Solomon built a high place for Chemosh the detestable idol of Moab, on the mountain which is east of Jerusalem, and for Molech the detestable idol of the sons of Ammon (1 Kings 11:4–8).

Because of this rebellion against God's statutes and commandments, God tore the kingdom from his hands, leaving the line of David only two tribes of Israel to govern (Judah and Benjamin).

The kings of the divided kingdoms continually led the people into the pagan practices of their neighbors. In fact, the northern kingdom had absolutely no kings who followed God, and even Judah had more evil kings than God-honoring kings. God sent many prophets to His people, with warnings and guidance, but they would not heed Him. The people sold themselves into "spiritual harlotry" and continually worshiped false gods and idols (see Israel's Spiritual Harlotry, page 72–73). In response, God brought judgment upon the people for their rebellion against Him and constant transgression of His law.

In 722 B.C., the Assyrians conquered the northern kingdom of Israel, and in 586 B.C. Judah fell to the Babylonians.

The physical kingdom of Israel would never be the same, even after the Jewish people returned to their homeland. But God has promised that one day He will fulfill all His promises for His people: to bring them back to their land and bestow His blessings upon them forevermore, for the glory of His name (Ezekiel 36:12, 22–28). He is not finished with the nation of Israel (Romans 11).

> "But this is the covenant which I will make with the house of Israel after those days," declares the LORD, "I will put My law within them and on their heart I will write it; and I will be their God, and they shall be My people" (Jeremiah 31:33).

Hezekiah's Tunnel

[701 B.C.]

During the reign of King Hezekiah, one of the greatest examples of water engineering was built beneath the city of Jerusalem in 701 B.C.

> Now the rest of the acts of Hezekiah — all his might, and how he made a pool and a tunnel and brought water into the city — are they not in the book of the chronicles of the Kings of Judah? (2 Kings 20:20; NKJV).

Hezekiah had the tunnel built in order to provide the city of Jerusalem with fresh water in case of a military siege.

The tunnel's source was the Gihon Spring. This natural spring could have been capable of supporting a population of 2,500 people. The tunnel itself follows an "S" shape and stretches 1,750 feet under Jerusalem, from the Gihon Spring to the Pool of Siloam. The tunnel was excavated from both sides, following a winding path, and met in the middle.

An inscription left by the workers, called the Siloam Inscription, was found in 1880 and reveals how the tunnel was cut out from the rock.

> . . . And this is the account of the tunneling through. While [the workmen raised] the pick each toward his fellow and while there [remained] to be tunneled [through, there was heard] the voice of the man calling to his fellow, for there was a split in the rock on the right hand and on [the left hand]. And on the day of the tunneling through the workmen stuck, each in the direction of his fellow, pick against pick. And the water started flowing from the source to the pool, twelve hundred cubits. And the height of the rock above the head of the workmen was a hundred cubits.

Read more on our blog:
geniusofancientman.blogspot.com

The Siloam Tunnel, or Hezekiah's Tunnel, is referenced in 2 Kings 20:20.

ISRAEL'S SPIRITUAL HARLOTRY – WORSHIPING OTHER GODS

God takes idolatry very seriously:

▷ The very first of the Ten Commandments Moses gave to the children of Israel at Sinai is: "You shall have no other gods before Me" (Exodus 20:3–6). It was a major part of the law (Lev. 19:1–4).

▷ He warns the Israelites not to follow the gods of the nations they conquer when they enter the Promised Land. This is why they had to annihilate everyone and destroy the plunder from each civilization (Exod. 34:10–17, Deut. 6:10–15, 7:1–5).

▷ It is an affront to His character and nature-"I am God and there is no one besides Me" (Is. 44:6, 8, 45:5–6, 14, 18, 21–22, 46:9 ff.) Also see: Isaiah 40:18–20.

Pagan god	Decription of Idol
Asherim/ Asherah	▷ Fertility goddess of the Canaanites. ▷ Worshiped on high places with sacred pillars. ▷ Male cult prostitutes associated with this goddess.
Ashtoreth	▷ Popular goddess in several cultures such as the Sidonians.
Baal	▷ Canaanite god of storm and justice; also the god of fertility and paired with Asherah. ▷ Pictured as a man standing on a bull. ▷ Many prophets and prostitutes associated with him.
Baal–Zebub/ Baal-Zebul	▷ The god of Ekron known as the "lord of the flies".
Chemosh	▷ National god of Moab and Ammon.
Molech	▷ Deplorable god and "abomination" of the Ammonites that required human sacrifice.
Milcom/ Malcalm	▷ Different than Molech; also an "abomination" of the Ammonites worshiped in Moab and Ammon.
Golden Calf/ Calves	▷ Molten image of a young cow, possibly connected to an Egyptian god.
Tammuz	▷ Syrian and Phoenician god of fertility. ▷ Part of the Babylonian false trinity.
Queen of Heaven	▷ Female deity of the skies that attracted worship from mainly women.
Host of Heaven	▷ Worship of the sun, moon, stars, and constellations.

Evidence of Idolatry

"They set for themselves sacred pillars and Asherim on every high hill and under every green tree" (2 Kings 17:10). Judg. 6:25–30; 1 Kings; 14:15; Isa. 27:9; Jer. 17:1–2

"because they have forsaken Me, and have worshiped Ashtoreth the goddess of the Sidonians..." (1 Kings 11:33). Judg. 2:11–14; 10:6

"So Israel joined themselves to Baal of Peor, and the LORD was angry against Israel" (Numbers 25:3). Deut. 4:3; Judg. 2:11–14; 1 Kings 16:31–32; 2 Chron. 28:2; Jer. 11:13; Hosea 2:8; Zeph. 1:4

"...So he sent messengers and said to them, "Go, inquire of Baal-zebub, the god of Ekron, whether I will recover from this sickness." (2 Kings 1:1-6)

"Then Solomon built a high place for Chemosh the detestable idol of Moab, on the mountain which is east of Jerusalem" (1 Kings 11:7). Jeremiah 48:7, 13, 46

"They built the high places of Baal that are in the valley of Ben-hinnom to cause their sons and their daughters to pass through the fire to Molech" (Jeremiah 32:35). 1 Kings 11:7; 2 Kings 16:3, 21:6; Jer. 7:31

For Solomon went after... Milcom the detestable idol of the Ammonites. (1 Kings 11:5) 1 Kings 11:33; Jer. 49:1–3; Zeph. 1:5

"They have made for themselves a molten calf, and have worshiped it and have sacrificed to it and said, 'This is your god, O Israel, who brought you up from the land of Egypt!'" (Exod. 32:8) 1 Kings 12:28–33; 2 Kings 10:29

"Then He brought me to the entrance of the gate of the LORD's house which was toward the north; and behold, women were sitting there weeping for Tammuz" (Ezek. 8:14).

"... and the women knead dough to make cakes for the queen of heaven; and they pour out drink offerings to other gods in order to spite Me" (Jer. 7:17–18). Jer. 44:15–19

"For he built altars for all the host of heaven in the two courts of the house of the LORD." (2 Kings 21:5) 2 Kings 17:16; Zeph. 1:5; Jer. 8:2

Assyria

[900–700 B.C.]

Israel was almost constantly under attack from the pagan nations surrounding it. As mentioned above, Assyria was one of the nations that conquered part of Israel, leading to its downfall. The Assyrians were among the most brutal civilizations to ever exist. The Assyrian Empire was descended from the early Akkadian Empire (one of two nations that formed out of Akkad). Even though the Assyrians formed a civilization right after the fall of Akkad, they did not rise to dominance until around 900–800 B.C., after which they became the strongest military power in the Middle Eastern world.

Power through Brutality

The Assyrian tactics for subduing their enemies were feared throughout the Middle East. When they conquered a nation they would make a show of brutality in order to dissuade anyone from trying to rebel. They would torture and execute people and burn cities to the ground to display their power.

Their horrifying practices included beheading, flaying of the flesh, dismembering victims, burning, and impaling on stakes.[2] They dehumanized and humiliated their prisoners. They inspired such fear that many nations, including the Egyptians, paid them monetary tribute to avoid destruction.

How and why would a civilization build itself upon such inhumane military characteristics? Apparently, the two principal tasks of an Assyrian king were to engage in military conquests and to build more structures. These were seen as religious duties and were accordingly obeyed with fervor. In the records that the Assyrians left behind, there is never mention of any lost battles. The kings were careful to always be represented as successful conquerors:

> The king, who acts with the support of the great gods his lords and has conquered all lands, gained dominion over all highlands and received their tribute, captures of hostages, he who is victorious over all countries.[3]

2 Erika Belibtreu, "Grisly Assyrian Record of Torture and Death," 1991, Biblical Archeology Society, online, http://faculty.uml.edu/ethan_Spanier/Teaching/documents/CP6.0AssyrianTorture.pdf, accessed October 16, 2014.
3 Albert Kirk Grayson, *Assyrian Royal Inscriptions, Part 2: From Tiglath-pileser I to Ashur-nasir-apli II* (Wiesbaden, Germany: Otto Harrassowitz, 1976), p. 165, http://faculty.uml.edu/ethan_Spanier/Teaching/documents/CP6.0AssyrianTorture.pdf. Accessed October 16, 2014

To suppress enemies was a divine task for these kings and to be victorious in battle proved that "the gods" were supporting them. More than just military conquests, it seems that the Assyrian kings continually attempted to outmatch one another in brutality. It became a badge of honor and pride to inflict suffering and devastation upon one's enemies and to be utterly feared because of it.

How did the Assyrians reach such a level of degradation?

Rejection of God	Worship of false deity	Obedience to deity in order to gain reward	Use laws from the deity to manipulate and gain power	Maintain power through sanction of deity	Control deity and assume complete authority	Self-deification

When the God of justice, grace, peace, and love is replaced with a false deity, the characteristics of God are replaced as well. When religion is not based upon the law and commandments of God, false beliefs have no standard from which to base right and wrong. The Assyrians became so entangled in their distorted beliefs that murder and torture became honorable. The kings were able to commit terrible acts in the name of religion and gave their god the credit for victory. They believed that by conquering other nations, they were also overcoming the gods of those nations. They were in fact asserting their own power over other gods. Through their brutality, the Assyrian kings guaranteed incredible fear and subjection from their enemies. They became like gods, controlling their empire with violence and severe punishment.

The same motive (god-like power and control) exists within some of the other great conquerors/rulers in history. When you look at men like Hitler, Stalin, Vlad the Impaler, Attila the Hun, Julius Caesar, Alexander the Great, Sennacherib, and Sargon the Great, you see one thing: a man who will go to any lengths for absolute power and control.

Above: Assyrian kings have rebels flayed as a warning to troublesome subjects.

Right: Assyrian warriors shown impaling Jewish prisoners

USED FOR GOD'S PURPOSE

Yet even with all their pagan ruthlessness, nations like Assyria were used to bring God glory and achieve His goals. God used Assyria to judge nations, particularly the nation of Israel. Ironically, while they thought their god Ashur was granting them victory, their success was actually according to the will of God (2 Kings 19:25). The Northern Kingdom of Israel was marked by decadence and rebellion and they clung to idolatry. They even went as far as sacrificing their children! Because of their immorality, God sent judgment upon them in the form of the Assyrian conquest.

Under the rule of King Sennacherib, the Assyrian Empire invaded Israel, conquering it rapidly and in the typical Assyrian fashion. After this conquest, the king deported the people who lived in Israel. This was one of the policies of the Assyrians, to deport people they conquered and then resettle subjects from a different area. This made rebellion unlikely because people were no longer living in their homelands. It was an effective system that the second Babylonian Empire would later adopt.

King Sennacherib of Assyria. Published in 1897 in the book titled *Peloubet's Select Notes A Commentary on the International Lessons for 1898.*

UNDER GOD'S JUDGMENT

In typical Assyrian tradition, Sennacherib continued his conquest after Israel and boasted that he would also conquer the Southern Kingdom of Judah, stating that their God could not save them:

> "Do you not know what I and my fathers have done to all the peoples of the lands? . . . Who was there among all the gods of those nations which my fathers utterly destroyed who could deliver his people out of my hand, that your God should be able to deliver you from my hand? . . . so the God of Hezekiah will not deliver His people from my hand." . . . They spoke of the God of Jerusalem as of the gods of the peoples of the earth, the work of men's hands (2 Chronicles 32:13–19).

Once again, a man was claiming to be greater than God, and as happened in other situations, God proved him wrong.

Sennacherib encamped his army around the city of Jerusalem during the days of King Hezekiah (see 2 Chronicles 32 and Isaiah 36–37). While he was besieging the city, God sent an angel down that killed 185,000 of his men. This forced Sennacherib to return to Assyria, defeated and unable to continue his conquest. Upon his return, his sons murdered him.

> Anytime man dares to openly mock and rebel against God, this is the typical result; even when it doesn't happen in his lifetime, the punishment for sin remains the same: death.

BABYLON

[700–550 B.C.]

Back in chapter five we discussed the first Babylonian empire led by Hammurabi. A second Babylonian empire arose much later, on the heels of the Assyrians. The second Babylonian Empire modeled itself upon the previous empire, the successful days of Hammurabi (1792–1750 B.C.). Babylon would soon outshine any empire that came before it. The great Babylonian king, Nebuchadnezzar, was one of the most impressive rulers to ever live, and he left a lasting legacy upon his death.

One of the Seven Wonders of the Ancient World was the Hanging Gardens of Babylon, shown here in Marten Heemskerck's painting; the Tower of Babel is in the background.

Nebuchadnezzar was almost solely responsible for bringing Babylon back to greatness. For many years, the nation had fallen from prominence, but under Nebuchadnezzar's rule they gained their former glory. They started their rise by defeating the current superpower, Assyria, and then overpowered all other threatening nations, until all were in subjection to them.

Under the rule of Nebuchadnezzar, the nation of Judah was conquered in 605 B.C. Nebuchadnezzar took the king of Judah captive along with other officials and stole many of the treasures from

the temple. Just as God used Assyria to judge the Northern Kingdom of Israel, Nebuchadnezzar was used by God to judge the people of Judah because they had disobeyed Him. This is a common theme throughout history; God ordains the rise and fall of all civilizations. Whether through the work of another nation or through seemingly "natural" disasters, when people rebel against God, judgment is assured (see chart on pages 38–39).

The Pride of Nebuchadnezzar

Nebuchadnezzar's achievements were great; he battled the strongest nations of his day and defeated them. He also strictly governed and maintained his empire throughout his reign.

However, Nebuchadnezzar made a grave mistake: he grew proud of his work and boasted of his achievements. Because he captured and worked with Israelite men like Daniel, Shadrach, Meshach, and Abednego, he knew who the true God was, and had seen evidence of His power in their lives. He even acknowledged God's power: "*How great are His signs and how mighty are His wonders! His kingdom is an everlasting kingdom and His dominion is from generation to generation*" (Daniel 4:3). And he was also given a vision and warning to break away from his sins and to recognize that God was the only supreme ruler of mankind (Daniel 4:19–27).

But Nebuchadnezzar ignored the warnings and continued to glorify himself saying, "Is this not Babylon the great, which I myself have built as a royal residence by the might of my power and for the glory of my majesty?" (Daniel 4:30).

And so God humbled Nebuchadnezzar: "Immediately the word concerning Nebuchadnezzar was fulfilled; and he was driven away from mankind and began eating grass like cattle, and his body was drenched with the dew of heaven until his hair

had grown like eagles' feathers and his nails like birds' claws" (Daniel 4:33).

After the Lord restored his sanity and throne, Nebuchadnezzar recognized God, blessed, praised, and honored Him (Daniel 4:34–37). He learned his lesson of humility, and the text of Daniel even indicates that he repented. God gave him wisdom to understand that "*[God's] ways are just, and He is able to humble those who walk in pride,*" (Daniel 4:37). Nebuchadnezzar's story is an amazing display of God's redemptive power.

A Prophetic Perspective

It was during the reign of Nebuchadnezzar that God gave descriptive and prophetic visions to both Nebuchadnezzar and the prophet Daniel concerning the rise and fall of several great kingdoms of the world. The prophecies in Daniel 2, 7, and 8 convey the futility of human world government and its offer to give mankind true security and happiness.

These prophecies are central in helping us understand God's view of man-made kingdoms and governments. He knows and establishes the rise and fall of every nation.

Four civilizations are described in the prophecies, each one falling to the next — none of them were lasting. In contrast, Daniel is told that a kingdom is coming that will never end!

> The God of heaven will set up a kingdom which will never be destroyed,
> and that kingdom will not be left for another people; it will crush and put an end to all these kingdoms, but it will itself endure forever (Daniel 2:44).

In this book we give you many examples of human efforts to conquer and control the world (or at least dominate as much as possible). In the Scriptures,

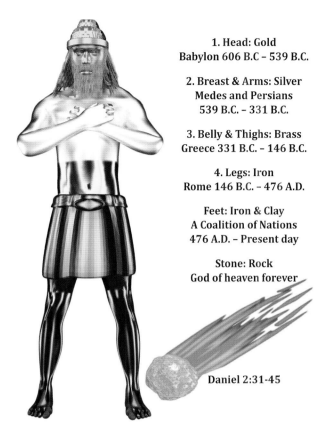

1. **Head: Gold**
Babylon 606 B.C – 539 B.C.

2. **Breast & Arms: Silver**
Medes and Persians
539 B.C. – 331 B.C.

3. **Belly & Thighs: Brass**
Greece 331 B.C. – 146 B.C.

4. **Legs: Iron**
Rome 146 B.C. – 476 A.D.

Feet: Iron & Clay
A Coalition of Nations
476 A.D. – Present day

Stone: Rock
God of heaven forever

Daniel 2:31-45

God uses these four kingdoms to illustrate the same thing: kingdoms rise and fall, characterized by their rebellion against God and their failure to endure.

The Four Kingdoms

In Daniel 2, Nebuchadnezzar had a dream and God gave him the interpretation through Daniel. It was a vision of a great statue consisting of different parts: a head of gold, a chest and arms of silver, its middle and thighs of bronze, legs of iron, and feet of part iron and part clay. According to the interpretation given to Daniel, the head of gold represented Nebuchadnezzar's kingdom of Babylon and the other materials were symbolic for three kingdoms that were yet to come.

Daniel also had a vision of four beasts (Daniel 7), which symbolized four kings, corresponding to the parts of the statue. From history we recognize the four kingdoms of both visions as Babylon, Mede-Persia, Greece, and Rome.

In another vision (Daniel 8), Daniel was actually given the names of two kingdoms that were to rise. In this vision he saw a ram that had two horns, one higher than the other. The angel Gabriel revealed that this ram represented the kings of Media and Persia. The kingdom would come in power and conquer all others. His vision also included a goat, which symbolized the rise of Greece. In his vision, the goat charged the ram and broke its horns (in ancient times horns were symbolic of power). The goat then became exceedingly great, but while he was strong, his horn was broken and four horns rose up to take its place. This passage clearly refers to Alexander the Great, perhaps the most successful conqueror in history.

Incredibly, when we look back and study these visions and the details that God revealed, we can see the different symbolic characteristics of the historic nations that were prophesied. God gave Daniel a glimpse into what was to come, though he did not comprehend it. Daniel was alarmed and astounded by the visions and what they revealed about God's view of man's kingdoms. Truly, God's perspective is far beyond our understanding. As Nebuchadnezzar declared, "*Surely your God is a God of gods and a Lord of kings and a revealer of mysteries*" (Daniel 2:47).

Wise men, Magicians, and Conjurers

The king of Babylon surrounded himself with dozens of men whom he expected would help him to rule. He employed magicians and astrologers who had great wisdom, knowledge, and understanding; they were also learned men, well educated and therefore honored. They could supposedly interpret dreams, tell the future, and provide counsel.

In Daniel 2, we read that Nebuchadnezzar was troubled by a dream and demanded his wise men to tell him both the dream and the interpretation; however, none of his pagan wise men were capable of performing this impossibility.

In contrast, when Daniel (one of the king's wise men) heard about the king's dream, he immediately prayed to God, who revealed both the dream and interpretation to Daniel. In response, Daniel affirms that all wisdom and power truly belong to God, not man:

> "It is He who changes the times and the epochs;
>
> He removes kings
> and establishes kings;
> He gives wisdom to wise men
> And knowledge to men of understanding.
>
> It is He who reveals the profound and hidden things;
> He knows what is in the darkness,
> And the light dwells with Him" (Daniel 2:21–22).

Gate of All Nations or Gate of Xerxes palace is in the ruins of Persepolis located today in Iran.

Mede-Persia
[550–330 b.c.]

The kingdom of Mede-Persia (known in secular history as simply "Persia") was one of the kingdoms that was prophesied in Nebuchadnezzar's dream. Represented by the chest and arms of silver in the statue, the Mede-Persians were not as magnificent as the Babylonians, but as symbolized by the conquering ram (in Daniel's vision), the Mede-Persian Empire was greater in power. It was during Daniel's life that they rose over the great Babylonian Empire and several other biblical figures served under this empire, including Nehemiah and Ezra.

Persia's greatest king, Cyrus the Great, enlarged the Persian Empire a great deal, and while he was a military genius, it was his political approach that garnered the most admiration. When he conquered regions, he made it seem like he was actually freeing them from their tyrannical rulers. This was confirmed by his custom of tolerance. Cyrus did not enslave his subjects; instead he tolerantly allowed his subjects to worship and live as they pleased. This was one of the first times a ruler practiced such methods in governance.[4]

bring loyalty from your people, but you will have no respect from your enemies.

Machiavelli demonstrates, through many examples from history, that the greatest leaders were those who achieved the balance of fear and love. Cyrus the Great was among these; his skill as a conqueror inspired fear and his stance on tolerance inspired a great love for him among his subjects.

Tomb of Cyrus the Great

The Art of Leadership

It is fascinating to study the art of leadership and the various approaches men take to achieve power. In one of the greatest literary works on the subject of leadership, *The Prince*, Niccolo Machiavelli wrote that there are two key elements that a leader must strive for to attain the loyalty of his people and the respect of his enemies: love and fear. Machiavelli stated that optimally, a balance of fear and love is best, but if a leader cannot achieve this balance the more important element is fear. Love will only

While many of the leaders we have studied thus far used force and brutality to achieve control over their subjects and enemies, Cyrus realized that he could secure loyalty through the unity brought by tolerance. However, as we will delve into later in this book, this view of tolerance leads us straight back to the unity seen at Babel.

Cyrus decided to live by a policy in which everyone's views are considered valid, and he became one of the greatest rulers in history. Today he is praised for his views of tolerance and described as a forward thinker in an age of extreme brutality. But he was simply repeating the worldview of Babel: a philosophy of unity ("come, let us . . .") and control through any means necessary.

4   Engineering an Empire: The Persians. Directed by Cannon, Mark. Performed by Peter Weller. United States: History Channel, 12/04/2006. TV series.

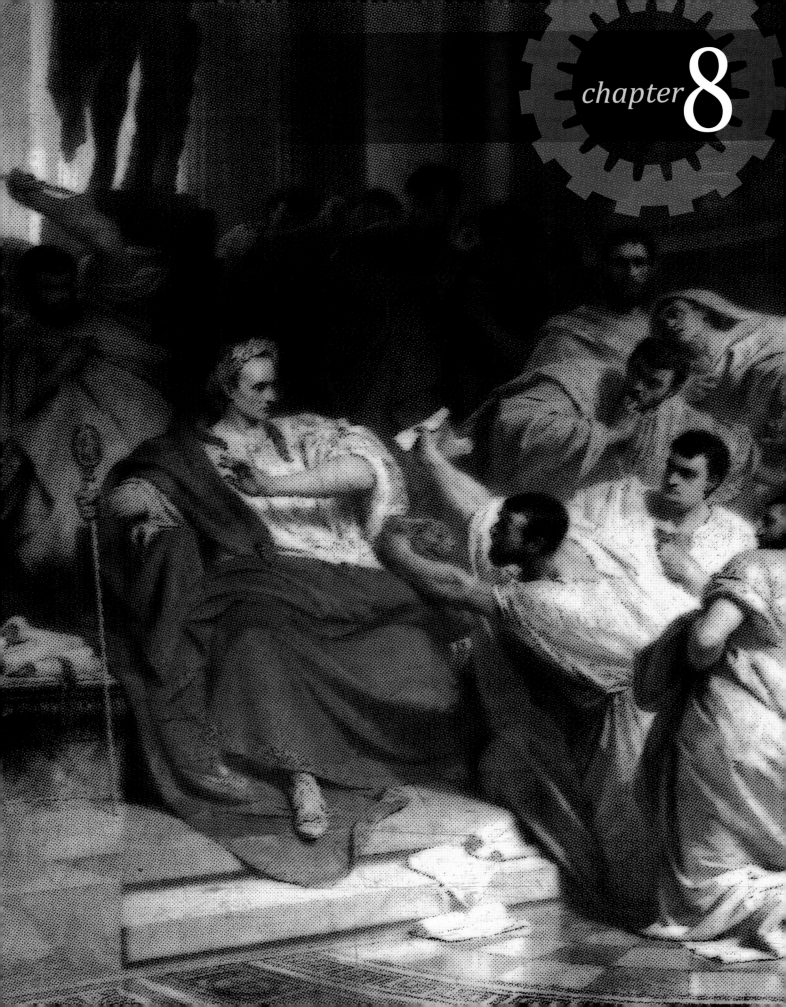

chapter 8

WORLD CONQUERORS

GREECE
[900–250 B.C. PEAK 500–300 B.C.]

Now we come to the civilization that many historians have called the "hinge" of advanced society: the Greeks. In many ways, they seemed to bring back and build upon knowledge and technology that was lost by many of the civilizations that came before them. The Greeks created incredible architecture, art, and inventions. There are aspects of their craftsmanship that we still cannot replicate!

PARTHENON

One example is the Greek Parthenon in Athens, Greece. The original was built in only nine years and completed in 438 B.C. Today, the *reconstruction* process has gone on for over 40 years, during which we have learned that our skill is far below that of the ancient Greeks! The famous pillars of the Parthenon were originally built with seamless connections between the blocks and each block was essentially the same. The indented curves were so precisely chiseled that even with all our modern technology we cannot reach the same quality as the master craftsmen who built it.[1]

CITY OF ALEXANDRIA, EGYPT

The city of Alexandria, a Greek city built in Egypt to honor Alexander the Great, is one massive display of ancient man's ability in the area of archaeoastronomy. The layout of the entire city was designed to be in alignment with the sun on the birthday of Alexander the Great. This type of archaeoastronomy on such a grand scale is truly amazing.[2]

When constructed, the Parthenon in Athens was dedicated to the goddess Athena. Even so, the building was used mainly as a treasury; it was a Christian church, and then a mosque before Greece became independent and removed all medieval and Ottoman buildings from the site in order to preserve it.

1   Zuk, Matthew. "The Genius of Ancient Man: Baffling Ancient Technology." The Genius of Ancient Man: Baffling Ancient Technology. September 4, 2013. Accessed May 11, 2015. http://geniusofancientman.blogspot.com/2013/09/baffling-ancient-technology.html.
2   Pappas, Stephanie. "Ancient Egypt City Aligned With Sun on King's Birthday" Live Science. www.livescience.com.http://www.livescience.com/23994-ancient-city-alexandria-sun.html (accessed May 11, 2015).

The Antikythera mechanism is dated at least 2,000 years old — created ahead of modern-day technology![3]

Recall the antikythera mechanism, one of the greatest examples of ancient technology that we discuss in *The Genius of Ancient Man*. Roughly the size of a shoebox, the antikythera mechanism has baffled historians with its incredible intricacy and design. Apparently it was able to predict the movements of the sun, moon, the 12 Zodiac signs, and maybe even the five planets the Greeks knew of. It tracked the Saros cycle (periods of solar and lunar eclipses), Metonic cycle (basis for the Greek calendar), and Callippic cycle (a lunar cycle that included four Metonic cycles), and perhaps even tracked the four-year cycle of the Olympic games.

Greek Theater in Athens, Greece

ALEXANDER THE GREAT

The nation of Greece was a powerful civilization before Alexander came along, but his rapid rise and astounding conquests launched him into a class of his own. Almost all of the great conquerors and generals who came after him compared their achievements to his. He was the bar that they all tried to reach. Alexander's rise was even prophesied in the Bible; the prophecy was so specific it even stated that four kingdoms would rise in his wake (Daniel 8:21–22).

However, like almost every other great conqueror and leader we have written of in this book, Alexander wanted to become greater, more powerful, and someone people would bow down to. He had an intense desire to make himself god and eventually he started claiming to be a half (demi) god. However, once he conquered half of Persia and Egypt, he found that several men who ruled these countries had also claimed to be gods. So during his time in Egypt he made it official, proclaiming that he was a full god among men, the son of Zeus-Ammon. He founded many cities bearing his own name to further his public image as a god.[4]

Alexander continued his conquest beyond Persia and Egypt, conquering all the way into India to the Indus River. He planned to go even farther, to China, but his men started to grumble. They had been at war for three years without seeing their homeland and they had had enough.

Alexander may have been one of the greatest human conquerors this world has ever known, but he was never content and was always striving for more. He was not known for tolerating other people's opinions and was quick to inflict severe punishment or death. He may have been successful at expanding his empire, but he was not well liked.

Many assassination attempts were made and Alexander died at age 33 in 323 B.C., most likely poisoned by one of his generals. Having no heirs, his kingdom was split among four men, just as was prophesied.

3   Landis, Don. *The Genius of Ancient Man: Evolution's Nightmare.* Green Forest, AR: Master Books, 2012. Pg 49.

4   Joshua J. Mark, "Alexander the Great," *Ancient History Encyclopedia*, November 13, 2013, http://www.ancient.eu/Alexander_the_Great/, accessed October 20, 2014.

THE EMPIRE OF ALEXANDER
334-323 B.C.

→ Conquest course of Alexander
✕ Battle
○ Siege
• Town founded by Alexander
⊙ Settlement of existing town
✕ Mountain pass
⊙ Greek colony
— Persian royal road
A Alexandria

0   500 km

Civilization of Philosophers

One of the most fascinating aspects of ancient Greek culture was their approach to "philosophy." It was very different than most other civilizations. They popularized the actual study of philosophical thought, and though they were not the true originators of their philosophical ideas, they identified and developed the worldviews that had been evident since the time of Babel. The great philosophers of Greece not only had an impact on their own culture, but also on those who would follow their legacy. Their influence continued long into the Roman Empire, and after the fall of Constantinople in A.D. 1453, the rediscovery of the Greek philosophers' works was one of the primary influences of the Renaissance and the following enlightenment period.

Relativism

Greek sophists were teachers who taught using philosophical dialogue and rhetoric (a form of argument and debate). They popularized the idea of *relativism*, believing that the concept of "truth" is relative to each individual. As Protagoras, a prominent leader of the movement, said, "What is true for you is true for you, but what is true for me is true for me."

According to relativism, many "facts" are simply "opinions," and contradictory truths are merely the product of differing perspectives (as a result of culture, upbringing, religion, etc.). Relativism concludes that there cannot be any absolute truth.

However, the logical conclusion of relativism is illogical; it refutes itself. If there is no absolute truth, then you cannot even state for certain that there is no absolute truth.

Idealism

There are many approaches to idealism, but the basic understanding of this philosophy is the belief that matter does not exist and all that we see, hear, touch, etc. is simply perceived in our mind. Therefore, reality only exists in the mind, and the senses are merely a way that the mind creates that reality.

Plato, one of the most famous philosophers of all time, affirmed this philosophy in his own particular way, known as dualism. Though he held that matter was real, he believed that it only existed because of the eternal ideas that are perceived by our rational souls.

However, idealism, as it is believed today, runs into problems when taken to its logical conclusion. For

Relativism	Everything is relative to each individual.	Truth is different for each person.	There is no absolute truth.	Man cannot know anything (even relativism) for certain.
Idealism	Matter doesn't exist — everything is in the mind.	Reality is relative to each person.	You are the only reality.	No basis for existence, let alone truth — no meaning in life.
Humanism	Man is the measure of all things.	Purpose is defined by man.	Man's goal is to pursue pleasure.	Selfishness and pride make man his own goal.

instance, how could we communicate with one another if reality was only in our mind? How could we discuss the world around us unless we all have the same perceived reality?

Some philosophers argue that everyone else is also a figment of the mind; other people are part of our own created reality. If so, we run into even more problems, for there is no longer absolute truth, there is no purpose for life, you have no basis for your existence, and you have no basis for anything else either. This philosophical thought descends into madness.

This philosophy is an incredible illustration of the intellectual insanity that results as a natural byproduct of man trying to erase God and His truth.

HUMANISM

Humanism was the most widespread philosophy of the Greeks. Even when they disagreed and debated concepts such as idealism, relativism, and naturalism, etc., they could almost always agree with this philosophy.

Humanism is well defined in a statement Protagoras made in the fifth century B.C.: "Man is the measure of all things: of things which are, that they are, and of things which are not, that they are not."[5]

A humanist raises up mankind and the individual, giving him authority and allowing him to define

purpose according to himself. It is a selfish philosophy that focuses on happiness and self-fulfillment. By erasing God and the concept of "gods" in general, you leave only yourself to serve.

This human-centered philosophy is the epitome of human arrogance in direct violation of God's commands. It is a philosophy that is prominent today and we can often find ourselves slipping into it. Every case of sin can be brought back to one original heart attitude that is characteristic of humanism: pride.

SOURCED IN BABEL

Relativism has its source in humanism and rejection of the truth of God's Word and God's authority. You can't believe in relativism and still believe in God, due to His absolute and immutable nature because God's nature is anti-relativistic.

Idealism came out of the thought process of rejecting a world created by God and creating our own reality.

Humanism was the very basis for the rebellion seen at Babel. The purpose of the people at Babel was to "make for ourselves a name."

All of these philosophies reject God and lead to only one place: absurdity and death.

> The fool has said in his heart, "There is no God" (Psalm 14:1).

---

5   https://answers.yahoo.com/question/index?qid=20101105084141AAQvtBo.

ROME
[300 B.C.–A.D. 400]

Rome. Perhaps the most famous of all ancient empires, the very name of Rome is associated with the concept of absolute power. Rome was the greatest and most powerful empire to ever exist, unmatched by any civilizations that preceded or succeeded it. The Romans built some of the most advanced structures known to mankind and produced some of the most innovative technology. Roman soldiers are considered to be the most brutally effective war machines in history. Rome dominated all other powers and controlled its lands with an iron fist; law and order were staples of the early Republic and the Empire.

All other empires are compared to Rome but no one has yet built an empire as vast and diverse as Rome or held it as long and completely as the Romans managed to.

Yet this incredible, incomparable empire couldn't last forever. It started to fall as political intrigue increased. By the time the Roman Empire dissolved, it had become one of the most decadent civilizations on the earth. Plagued by internal strife and power-plays, it quickly began to collapse.

ROME'S BEGINNINGS

Rome started out as a small, seemingly insignificant city-state. It began its rise through defensive wars, raising armies from the peasants and farmers surrounding the city. It eventually began to conquer its neighboring enemies and add more land to its growing nation.

Rome came into conflict with the Carthaginians and, after many years of frequent battles, finally defeated them in 146 B.C. Thereafter they became the sole superpower of the Mediterranean, but their borders didn't change drastically for another 80 years. The great emperors that set the Romans apart were still to come. Rome wouldn't become the great power it is famous for until a certain man came to power, a man who would change Rome forever, a man who would be proclaimed a god.

Highly-detailed relief in marble from the Ludovisi Battle sarcophagus found near the ancient walls of Rome, depicts a Roman battle with the Goths. The central figure is believed to represent Hostillian, the younger son of Roman Emperor Decius.

JULIUS CAESAR

Gaius Julius Caesar, commonly known as Julius Caesar, was one of history's greatest commanders. Though his political ability was lacking, during his time as Roman Consul he conquered much of Europe. He expanded the republic to include all of Gaul (modern-day France) as well as part of Germany. He conducted the first invasions into Britain and conquered the southern portion of the island.

His co-consul, Gnaeus Pompeius Magnus (known as Pompey the Great), was his only rival and they soon came into conflict with each other as they vied for leadership of the Roman state. In 49 B.C., civil war began as the two greatest Roman commanders were pitted against each other. Finally, Julius Caesar defeated the great Pompey after warring throughout the Republic, from Greece, to Spain, to Africa, and to Egypt. After being cornered in Egypt, Pompey was assassinated by the Egyptians, who hoped to gain Caesar's favor.

Caesar returned to Rome and prepared to make himself emperor, transitioning Rome from a republic to an empire. However, this was not to be. In one of the most legendary assassinations, Caesar was betrayed by the Senate, and the great Roman commander was killed. His death sparked yet another series of civil wars, as men fought for control of Rome. In the end, through wars, betrayals, and the death of his rivals, Caesar's adopted son, Octavian, managed to secure the throne. In the process, he added both Egypt and Israel to the new empire. Rome was greater than ever.[6]

6   Collins, Stephen Dando. Caesar's Legion: The Epic Saga of Julius Caesar's Elite Tenth Legion and the Armies of Rome. Hoboken, NJ: John Wiley & Sons, Inc, 2002.

AUGUSTUS (OCTAVIAN)

After the end of the second civil war, Octavian began to settle things in Rome and would eventually be counted as the greatest politician to ever live. He had the support of the Senate and quickly began to make preparations for the creation of an empire.

Somehow Octavian was able to appear as a humble ruler who was not really an emperor, while maintaining complete control over the republic. In 29 B.C. his reign officially began and his name was eventually changed to Augustus, meaning "great" or "venerable," and he also took the title of "first citizen." These were innocent-sounding labels but they indicated absolute power.

Augustus set up a brilliant foundation for government and his reign was marked by the least internal strife of all Roman emperors; none are considered to be greater than him. From a political standpoint, he was brilliant, shrewd, and one of the best rulers in history. However, from a moral standpoint, he was no model of excellence.

Augustus, like other rulers before him, sought to control his people through religion. He recognized it would create more patriotism among the Romans and, as a result, there would be fewer rebellions. Then, in a clever move, he added Julius Caesar to the Roman pantheon of gods! He never asked for deification himself, but that was clearly his goal. After all, he was the heir to the great Julius Caesar, and the leader of the great Roman Empire. He also added "Divi Filius" to his name, meaning "Son of the Divine,"[7] but he only gained the status of godhood after his death.

Augustus' legacy would continue throughout time; the empire he started would survive for hundreds of years, in spite of being plagued by terrible leaders. Somehow it managed to stay afloat even during the reigns of some of the worst rulers in history.

CALIGULA

Caligula (ruled A.D. 37–41)[8] is considered to be one of the worst Roman emperors to ever grace the throne. He was one of the most decadent rulers and nearly brought the empire to ruin. He was the first of any Roman emperor to claim godhood while still alive and even ordered that a statue of himself be placed in every temple, including the Jewish temple in Jerusalem. This very nearly resulted in a rebellion, but Caligula didn't care in the slightest. His pride was not as calculated or shrewd as that of Augustus. In contrast, he took the route of madness and wickedness, thinking he was untouchable. He believed that, as the emperor of the Roman Empire, he should be worshiped and obeyed as a god. Instead, his own Praetorian Guard assassinated him.

NERO

Nero (ruled A.D. 54–68) was essentially as bad as Caligula. He too claimed godhood during his lifetime, and it was during his reign that the Romans began to mercilessly persecute Christians. His disgustingly immoral lifestyle, along with crimes such as murdering his mother, executing hundreds of Christians, and possibly destroying much of Rome, mark him as one of the empire's worst rulers.

He was known to have burned Christians alive as torches at his garden orgies. He initiated the arena games where animals tore Christians to pieces and where mass crucifixions took place. Under his rule, both Peter and Paul, the Apostles, were executed in Rome. Like Caligula before him, Nero's lack of morals and his belief that he should be unquestionably worshiped and obeyed ultimately led to his demise. The empire revolted in A.D. 68 and his guard deserted him. He reportedly decided to commit suicide but lacked the courage and so forced his servant to help him.[9]

But Rome was also marked by several emperors who were more like Augustus than like Caligula and Nero. These men include Vespasian, Trajan, and Hadrian. Each of them took the route of order instead of indulgence.

7   "Son of God and Ancient Coins," http://ejc-nexus.net/AMBS-Handouts/Jn1.1-18-SonofGodandAncientCoins.pdf, accessed October 24, 2014.

8   "Gaius Caesar Germanicus," http://www.biography.com/people/caligula-9235253, accessed October 20, 2014.

9   "Nero," http://www.biography.com/people/nero-9421713, accessed Oct 20, 2014.

VESPASIAN

Choosing to earn respect instead of demand it, Vespasian (ruled A.D. 69–79) brought Rome back from the brink of destruction after Nero's reign. He reintroduced order and began the construction of the most iconic building of Rome: the Colosseum.

Construction began in A.D. 72 and it was paid for by the precious metals and materials stolen from Jerusalem's temple in A.D. 70. To build the magnificent structure, 12,000 Jewish captives were taken from Israel and brought to Rome. More than 6,000 tons of concrete were used, along with huge blocks from a quarry 20 miles away. The construction was completed eight years later and the colossal building rose to a height of 160 feet and stretched 620 feet long and 513 feet wide, making it the largest and tallest Roman building ever.

The Colosseum could hold more than 70,000 people with ease; they even had tickets that designated seating much like we do today. It was built with 110 drinking fountains and two large restrooms to accommodate the fans. They even built a retractable roof, which could be raised and adjusted to control light and air flow. The most astonishing part of the Colosseum was that the arena could be flooded to host the naval gladiatorial battles. Water was brought in from a nearby aqueduct and then pipes were built to expel the water to the city's sewage system. The entire building was a masterpiece and is still a wonder today.[10]

10 Engineering an Empire: Rome. Directed by Cassel, Christopher. Performed by Peter Weller. United States: History Channel, 09/13/2005. TV series.

HADRIAN

When Hadrian came to power (ruled A.D. 117–138) he set about securing the massive Roman Empire. He also built some of Rome's most imposing structures, including the Pantheon and Hadrian's Wall.

Hadrian's wall stretched 73 miles across the entire island of Britain, from coast to coast. It was built along very rugged terrain and often used cliffs and natural barriers to aide in its defense. It was 15 feet high with parapets rising 6 feet higher. A 9-foot ditch was dug at its base to deter enemy invaders, and a 120-foot ditch with earthen walls was built behind it as a backup, in case any invaders made it past the stone wall itself. It was the largest stone fortification built by the Romans. Every mile, a guard post was built that housed 60 Roman soldiers, and between each guard post, two watchtowers allowed Roman troops to keep an eye on the natives. Seventeen large forts were also built along the wall, each able to hold up to a thousand Roman soldiers. It was constructed in an astonishing five years and provided both a physical and psychological wall to deter invaders.

Hadrian is also credited with rebuilding the Pantheon in A.D. 126. It was built as a temple for all of the gods and is most famous for its rotunda. Built in a perfect circle stretching 150 feet high and 150 feet wide, it didn't require any buttresses or columns for support. It had the largest unsupported dome in the world for over a thousand years. In order to hold up the massive ceiling, the Romans built a solid base of walls 20 feet thick. They also thinned out

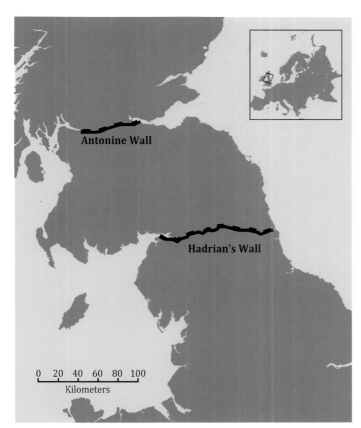

Antonine Wall

Hadrian's Wall

0 20 40 60 80 100
Kilometers

the amount of material used on the ceiling as they went upward, and recessed (indented) panels were built into the dome to make it lighter and more decorative. They also built the "oculus," a 30-foot wide hole in the center of the ceiling, to lighten it and help deal with the tremendous stress the dome had on the structure. The oculus also provided incredible lighting inside the dome to honor the gods.[11]

Hadrian was known as a tolerant and wise ruler throughout most of his reign, but in his later years he began to persecute people who opposed him. Even though he always claimed that emperors should be obeyed out of love, he began to use fear to control the country and the senate. Before his death, he forced the senate to agree to the names of the next two emperors; fortunately, both went on to become very successful.[12]

A Legacy of Rulers

One aspect that unites all of Rome's rulers was the insatiable desire to become great and to be remembered. From Julius Caesar to Constantine (an emperor who moved the capital of the empire to Constantinople — modern-day Istanbul), Rome was a birthplace for men with aspirations of preeminence. The desire to control and to leave a legacy of power was a mark of Roman dominance. With all her supremacy and prestige, Rome produced some of the greatest and also some of the worst rulers to ever live.

The fall of Rome is among the hardest dates to decipher because the "true" date of its fall is uncertain. There are several options that various historians support:

▷ When Constantine moved the capital to his newly constructed city, Constantinople, in A.D. 330, the focus was shifted away from the city of Rome, and the emperors no longer ruled from there.

▷ One could say Rome fell when it was sacked by the Visigoths in A.D. 410, then by the Vandals in A.D. 455, and one last time by the Ostrogoths in A.D. 546.

▷ Some would consider the "Byzantine Empire" as the Roman Empire, and if that was the case then, the Byzantine Empire didn't fall until A.D. 1453 when the Ottomans sacked Constantinople.

Regardless of when exactly Rome fell, its influence continued. The bishop (of Catholic Christianity) in Rome quickly rose in dominance over the Church after the empire had faded. He became known as the pope and wielded incredible power over any nation that claimed to be Christian. The papacy began to have authority over most of Europe, and in A.D. 800, the Holy Roman Empire was established, with Charlemagne as its first emperor.

So even though Rome is a relic of the past, its influence carried on and is felt even to this day.

11 Ibid.
12 "Emperor Hadrian," http://spartacus-educational.com/ROMhadrian.htm, accessed October 20, 2014.

INCREDIBLY ADVANCED ROMAN TECHNOLOGY

Many of the discoveries of ancient technology have confounded modern historians; however, this one might be the most astounding. The Lycurgus Cup first came to light in the 1950s and immediately puzzled archaeologists. The 1,600-year-old cup actually *changes color* based on where light hits it. It looks green if the light comes from the front, and red if light shines from behind it.[13]

Researchers now know how the Romans did it: nanotechnology! The Romans were apparently far better craftsmen than originally thought! The cup's mysterious features are caused by impregnating tiny particles of gold and silver into the glass. The Romans were somehow able to crush and grind the gold and silver to the molecular scale, 50 nanometers in diameter. That's more than a thousand times smaller than a grain of table salt! Not only that, but due to the precise mixture of the precious metals, it seems the Romans knew exactly what they were doing and created the cup for a specific purpose.[14] It is truly astounding! Never before has advanced technology of this scale been discovered in an ancient artifact; not even the Antikythera mechanism (page 84) compares.

But the astonishment does not end there. Scientists have replicated the technology of the chalice in order to run more tests. They discovered that the nanotechnology of the cup works as follows: when hit with light, the electrons in the cup vibrate in a way that makes the chalice appear a certain color depending on the observer's position. If liquid was in the cup it would change the vibrations, which would thereby change the color of the cup. The prototype that the scientists created (for preservation purposes the original cup cannot be tested) was 100 times more sensitive to different salt levels in liquids than current commercial sensors with similar technology.[15] Such a detection mechanism would have been very handy for the Romans — they may have been able to tell if someone was trying to poison their ruler!

Modern scientists are still studying this cup because even today we can learn and improve our own technology based on methods used 1,600 years ago!

Practical Applications

Life as a citizen of the Roman Empire could be a comfortable one, either in the home or workplace, and a very effective one on the battlefield. Much is commonly known about the empire's public baths, aqueducts, and architectural wonders, but there are countless other innovations from glassworking to hydraulic mining, that demonstrate the role technology played in the daily lives of Romans. These include: Pozzolana cement or concrete, cranking tools, brass coins, treadwheel cranes, arch-gravity dams, force pumps as part of a fire engines, water organs, floor and wall heating systems called hypocausts, hydrometers, saw mills, grain mills, oil presses, gilding with mercury, simple stone or metal official daily notices like a newspaper called *Acta Diurna,* odometers, early reaper, wood veneer, street maps, boarding bridges for naval battles, and much more. Many examples are ones that other cultures adopted later in history and some we continue to perfect or hope to duplicate today.

The practical application of technology and innovation is one reason that the Roman Empire became so successful. Not only did Roman craftsmen create new ways of doing things, but the empire also served as a vehicle to absorb and widely distribute other technology throughout its far-flung borders.

13 Zeeya Merali, "This 1,600-Year-Old Goblet Shows that the Romans Were Nanotechnology Pioneers" *Smithsonian Magazine*, http://www.smithsonianmag.com/history-archaeology/This-1600-Year-Old-Goblet-Shows-that-the-Romans-Were-Nanotechnology-Pioneers-220536661.html, accessed September 3, 2013.
14 Ibid.
15 Ibid.

Roman surgical tools discovered at
the ruins of Pompeii

The Romans used treadmill cranes. Here is a depiction of a double
treadwheel crane in Pieter Bruegel's *The Tower of Babel.*

One practical and industrial Roman application for the
lever was in moving marble.

A suggested improvement in the fourth century,
De Rebus Bellicis, for ox-powered Roman paddleboats;
it is not known if such a craft was ever built.

The sestertius was a small Roman coin. During the
Roman Republic it was silver, and during the Roman
Empire, it was larger and bronze.

Artificial leg made from
bronze plates attached to
a wooden core, found in a
tomb near Capua.

One of the greatest architectural works of Rome is the Colosseum. Its outer wall is estimated to have used over 3,531,467 cubic feet of travertine stone held together with iron clamps rather than mortar. In addition to the arena and interior seating, it also has a series of tunnels and cages beneath the arena called the hypogeum.

As civil engineers, the Roman Empire was almost without compare. They built extensive public projects including aqueducts like this one in southern France that used gravity to bring water to cities for use in toilets, fountains, public baths, and other useful purposes that helped minimize sanitation problems without limiting water use.

An example of the Roman bath houses; this one is located in Bath, England. It took advantage of hot springs in the area.

Hypocausts (above and below) were located below the floors; interior walls had spaces left so that the hot air from the furnace in the hypocaust system could move upward, heating along the way.

chapter 9

CIVILIZATIONS OF THE NEW WORLD

As we journey to the Americas, you will notice that the ancient civilizations don't seem quite so ancient. They appeared so much later than those in the Middle East, Europe, India, China, etc. that we tend to view them as less intelligent and less impressive. However, as discussed on page 19, civilizations experienced a much slower growth in the Americas simply because it took so much longer for the dispersed people to reach their final destinations. These people groups became isolated from the rest of the world, inhibiting trade and communication. Populations were smaller and therefore their ability to build large structures, advance in technology, and rise in power was also hindered as the civilizations slowly matured, unlike the quick rise of the nations near Babel.

It is almost as if the American civilizations were on their own separate timeline from the others. They would have continued along and progressed in a similar way if not for the collision of the two worlds in A.D. 1492, when Christopher Columbus reached America. As world exploration, conquest, and colonization increased, the American civilizations, though competent and advanced for their circumstances, were misunderstood and abused by the arrival and invasion of foreign forces.

MAYA — GOLDEN AGE

[A.D. 250–900]

The Golden Age of the Mayans is generally believed to be around A.D. 250, though the civilization was flourishing centuries earlier than that. It was during this "Classic Period" that the Mayans built most of their famous cities and temples in their large territory covering the entire Yucatan Peninsula, Guatemala, and Belize, as well as parts of Mexico and Honduras. The Maya are well known for their ritual ball games, amazingly accurate calendar, early system of writing, and deeply religious culture. The

An example of a Mayan glyph; Mayans conveyed meaning with the glyphs that could represent a whole word or part of a word.

civilization was ruled by kings known as "kuhul ajaw" or "holy lords" who claimed to be related to the gods and served as mediators between the gods and the people of earth.[1]

The Maya were one of the most dominant societies of Mesoamerica and yet, for reasons unknown, they abandoned their incredible cities between the eighth and ninth centuries, and by the time the Europeans arrived, the remaining Maya were settled in small, scattered agricultural villages.[2]

Mayan empire

1   "Maya," http://www.history.com/topics/maya, accessed October 21, 2014.
2   Ibid.

El Mirador archaeological site, El Petén, Guatemala

Mayan bird man

EL MIRADOR

The enormous, ancient city of El Mirador (three times the size of downtown Los Angeles!) is one of the greatest enigmas of the Mayan civilization. It was built hundreds of years before the "Classic Maya Period" and yet it displays advanced architecture and housed up to 200,000 people.[3] The existence of El Mirador and the discovery of its antiquity has made archaeologists reexamine how the Mayan culture progressed. They were not slow to develop organizational, technical, and artistic abilities — they had them all along!

El Mirador is also home to the largest discovered pyramid in the world (by volume). The La Danta complex is more than 230 feet high and covers almost 45 acres.[4] The excavation process is still continuing and it may be some time before this massive pyramid is fully released from the subtropical jungle that has hidden it for 2,000 years.

Elsewhere at El Mirador, an incredible discovery was made: the earliest known Mayan creation myth, predating others by over a thousand years! It was found carved on two panels, 26 feet long and 20 feet high. The images of monsters, gods, and two twins swimming back from the underworld exactly corroborates the text of the *Popol Vuh*, a sacred book of Mayan myths, history, traditions, and their creation story.[5] The *Popul Vuh* was first transcribed and translated in the 16th century by Father Ximenez (a Dominican priest), and many historians asserted that the Spanish contaminated the *Popol Vuh* with the influences of Catholicism. However, now it has been confirmed that the key parts of the *Popol Vuh* are indeed accurate representations of Mayan mythology. The Mayan account of creation was well established for thousands of years before the Spanish arrived!

The temple atop the pyramid

---

3   Chip Brown, "El Mirador, the Lost City of the Maya," *Smithsonian Magazine* (May 2011), http://www.smithsonianmag.com/history/el-mirador-the-lost-city-of-the-maya-1741461/, accessed October 21, 2014.

4   Ibid.

5   Ibid.

POPUL VUH CREATION STORY

(Translation by Allen J. Christianson. 2007 *Popol Vuh: Sacred Book of the Quiché Maya People.* Electronic version of original 2003 publication.)[6]

This is the account of when all is still silent and placid. All is silent and calm. Hushed and empty is the womb of the sky. These, then, are the first words, the first speech. There is not yet one person, one animal, bird, fish, crab, tree, rock, hollow, canyon, meadow, or forest. All alone the sky exists. The face of the earth has not yet appeared. . . . Nothing stirs. All is languid, at rest in the sky. . . . Only the expanse of the water, only the tranquil sea lies alone. There is not yet anything that might exist. All lies placid and silent in the darkness, in the night.

All alone are the Framer and the Shaper, Sovereign and Quetzal Serpent, They Who Have Borne Children and They Who Have Begotten Sons. Luminous

Quetzal Serpent

they are in the water, wrapped in quetzal feathers and cotinga feathers. Thus they are called Quetzal Serpent. In their essence, they are great sages, great possessors of knowledge. Thus surely there is the sky. There is also Heart of Sky, which is said to be the name of the god.

The account goes on to describe how the god "Heart of Sky," in partnership with his fellows, speaks into existence the dry land, the mountains, the animals, and finally mankind, to worship them.

THE SIGNIFICANCE OF CREATION ACCOUNTS

Every religion has some form of creation or origin account. From pantheistic religions to beliefs like evolution, every culture has to come up with some way to explain the origin of the things we see.

Certainly, today evolution is among the most popular, but in the ancient times there were many different stories and traditions. While some don't seem to bear any resemblance to the true creation account recorded in Scripture, others are quite close to it.

Mankind knows his own finiteness and we question where we came from. We want to know our origin. The intriguing aspect of most of the ancient creation myths is their similarity. Most are clear distortions of the same account that is recorded for us in the Bible. They confirm the truth of God's Word and also serve as evidence that mankind once knew the true story, but over time and due to the Dispersion, the stories were altered and became more fiction than fact.

If you read and study the different creation accounts, the perversions of Satan will become evident, as well as the deliberate tampering of man in an attempt to rewrite history for his own purposes. Yet the best lies are the ones that contain a nugget of truth, and it is fascinating to recognize the scraps of fact hidden in the myths.

---

6 Mesoweb: www.mesoweb.com/publications/Christenson/PopolVuh.pdf.)

The enigmatic El Castillo pyramid at the center of Chichen Itza. When it was excavated in 1935, an offering site with a Chac Mool, or reclining figure, was found and the following year, a red jaguar statue with jade inlays for spots and white-painted flint teeth was uncovered.

CHICHEN ITZA

Located in southeast Mexico, Chichen Itza is one of the largest Mayan cities ever discovered. It was likely built around A.D. 600, but only became an important regional capital later in A.D. 800–900. Chichen Itza means "at the mouth of the well of the Itza," which referred to the large natural sinkholes that would have provided the "Itza" people with precious water. One of these holes is famously known as the "Well of Sacrifice," where it is known that the Maya offered treasures and sacrificed human beings to the rain god by casting them into the well.[7]

Chichen Itza is also home to some of the greatest feats of archaeoastronomy in the world. Astronomy was a significant focus of Mayan society, and astronomical characteristics are commonly found in their architecture.

El Castillo, "The Castle," is the central structure of the city. It looms at an impressive 79 feet, and is famous for an event that occurs twice a year, at the spring and fall equinoxes. At these times, the setting sun creates a snaky shadow along the stairs. The shadow makes its way down the pyramid toward the snakehead sculptures at the bottom. The engineering required to produce such an effect is astounding.[8]

The Mayans also built "El Caracol," known as "The Observatory," to track the movements of the planet Venus. A difficult planet to track, it appears in the morning only to disappear all day until it emerges again in the evening. These movements were so deceptive that even the Greeks believed it was two different celestial bodies. But the Mayans were not so deceived.[9]

7   "Chichen Itza: The Central Yucatan Peninsula," http://www.zuko.com/CrypticSphere/ Lost_Civilizations_Chichen_Itza.asp, aAccessed October 31, 2014.

8   "Ancient Observatories: Chichen Itza," http://www.exploratorium.edu/ancientobs/chichen/ HTML/castillo.html, accessed July 2, 2013.
9   Ibid.

ASTRONOMY

While astronomy was an important aspect to many cultures worldwide, the Maya were particularly enthralled with the study of the heavens. The movement of the celestial bodies was intertwined with everything they did, from their architecture to their religious ceremonies, to their very livelihoods.

All of their chief structures were built with archaeoastronomical characteristics. Their incredible calculations of the solstices, equinoxes, and half-quarter days are astounding. Their ability to track major planets was unparalleled even by the Greeks!

They also studied astronomy for religious purposes, and each of their deities were marked in the sky. They believed that through the sky they could make predictions of the future. It was believed that understanding the cycles of the night sky would allow them to predict what the gods would do. This led to the creation of things like the Mayan Calendar and Codex, aids in predicting the future.

The desire to understand the night sky led them to advance the study of mathematics, and they also used their astronomical knowledge to determine agricultural cycles (when to plant, harvest, and prepare seeds).

Ironically, their obsession with the night sky, which they thought would allow them to predict the future, did not actually keep their empire from collapsing. For some reason, still unknown to historians, the power of the Maya was broken. They abandoned their great cities and scattered throughout the region, living thereafter in small villages dependent on farming.

The serpent detail or theme is often found in the stonework of the Maya as it is here at the complex of Chichen Itza.

MISSISSIPPIAN CIVILIZATION
A.D. 700–1300

North American civilizations are often overlooked when studying ancient history, yet there were several incredible civilizations that arose and are worth noting.

The Mississippians were a North American civilization that flourished early in history. They settled in the fertile bottomland surrounding the Mississippi River for centuries before the arrival of the European explorers. At their center was the metropolis at Cahokia, a large city boasting massive earthen mounds, an organized government, and evidence of amazing archaeoastronomy. The Mississippians were known for their mound building, like many other early American people, and left their distinctive mark on the landscape with various earthenworks in different shapes and sizes.

Cahokia was abandoned around A.D. 1400 for unknown reasons, and the Mississippian culture collapsed by the 1500s.

Mississippian and Related Cultures

Sheffield
Mero
Red Wing
Point Saubie
Cambria
Overton
Midway Village
Meadow
Aztalan
Carcajou Point
Mills Village

Oneota

Dickson
Sunwatch
Port Ancient
Cloverdale
Hahns Field
Baum
Feurt
BBB Motors
Fox Farm
Hobson
Sponemann
Cahokia
Clay Mound
Tolu
Angel
Annis
Wickliffe
Kincaid
Corbin
Towasahgy
Castalian Springs
Middle Mississippian
Sellars
Obion
Mound Bottom
Citico
Town Creek
Spiro
Parkin
Shiloh
Nacooches
Caddoan Mississippian
Chucalissa
Hobbs
Florence
Island
Etawah
Rembert
Menard-Hodges
Mason's Plantation
Battle Mound
Winterville
Bessemer
Ocmulgee
Belcher
Holly Bluff
Moundville
Irene
Caddoan Mounds
Gahagan
South Appalachian Mississippian
Emerald
Plaolemine
Battle Creek
Lake Jackson
Medora
Fort Walton
Letchworth

Replica of a hut and the mound at Cahokia Mounds State Historic Site

Monks Mound at the Cahokia Mounds State Historic Site

Anasazi
[A.D. 800–1200 Golden Age 900–1130]

The Anasazi people of the Southwest, for instance, left a lasting impression that is still being investigated today. They settled in the Four Corners region of the United States where Colorado, Utah, Arizona, and New Mexico meet. The Navajo named them "Anasazi," meaning "ancient enemies," but today they are often referred to as "Ancient Puebloans" after their most probable descendants.

The Anasazi and their incredible yet inexplicably abandoned architecture pose a great mystery to archaeology. They left behind no written records, only the convoluted and conflicting accounts of oral tradition. Some claim the Anasazi appeared as early as 100 B.C. as the basket-weaving tribes that wandered the South; however, the appearance of the organized and settled civilization known for its farming and amazing cliff dwellings wasn't truly established until around A.D. 700.[10]

The Anasazi were more than mere hunter-gatherers turned farmers. They successfully developed a political empire with traces of Babel-influenced religion, astronomy, and social practices. The wandering tribes of warring people came together and created a network of villages, trade centers, and sacred places.

At the height of the Anasazi civilization, population growth was exploding and trade was flourishing. In the center of Anasazi life, Chaco Canyon (in present day northwest New Mexico) became the hub of trade for the entire region. Numerous towns were constructed in the area as well as the remarkable "Great Houses."

The largest and most well known of these Great Houses is called Pueblo Bonito. It covers over two acres and incorporates at least 650 rooms among its five stories! Some archaeologists now believe that Pueblo Bonito was not a city but rather a ritual center. This is because the surrounding cliffs and the architecture of the structure are marked with petroglyphs of the solar and lunar cycles.

Documented sites of the Anasazi ruins in relation to sites for the Mogollon and Hohokam cultures.

10 "Population Change," *Land Use History of North America*, http://cpluhna.nau.edu/People/population_change.htm, accessed October 6, 2014.

Interior view of a kiva, and below,
the exterior entrance

POLYTHEISTIC PANTHEISM

The small subterranean structures known as "kivas" are a plentiful feature of Anasazi sites. Kivas have long been considered to have served a religious and ceremonial purpose. These round buildings were usually aligned with the cardinal directions and celestial events.

Like many Native American tribes, the Anasazi believed in a sort of polytheistic pantheism, which allowed them to deify animals and plants as spirits and yet worship only one creator god of whom the spirits were a part. This "major spirit" is sometimes called "the Creator"; sometimes it is depicted as the sun, and sometimes the people referred to it as "the Grandmother."

In any case, communication with the spirits was essential for the Anasazi people. The spirits were responsible for bringing rain, healings, harvest, and almost everything else as well. For this reason, shamanism was probably an important aspect of Anasazi life. Shamans could be chosen at an early age; children were associated with spiritual connections if they had deformities, seizures, and/or hallucinations. The shamans would connect the people to spirits, whom they considered both good and bad, and intercede and inquire on behalf of the tribe. The process used to enter into visions and communication with the spirit world (divination) included intoxicants, hypnotic chanting, dancing, and pain. It is also known that many ancient native peoples used hallucinogenic drugs to induce trances (such as the Datura plant). Connecting with the

spirit world through visions required breaking down mental barriers and disconnecting from the physical world.

Other "spiritual leaders" in ancient Pueblo history were venerated because of family lineage, initiation into religious societies, or their possession of secret knowledge. Some were thought to have special communication with the spirits through their profession or personal character.[11]

11 "Who were the Anasazi?" http://www.blm.gov/co/st/en/fo/ahc/who_were_the_anasazi.
   html, accessed October 6, 2014.

104

CANNIBALISM IN CHACO

One of the appalling subjects of discussion regarding the Anasazi is the indication and evidence of close to 50 cases of cannibalism in the nation. The topic is highly disputed, with some experts saying it appears to have been a common practice and others claiming it never happened at all.

Evidence consists of mutilated human remains, splintered and charred bones, and even bones that appeared to have been boiled. At one site, a small village in Colorado, evidence of two victims was found. The disarticulated bodies missing arms and feet, and bones displaying cut marks eerily similar to those found on butchered animals, have led archaeologists to believe that two young males were killed and likely consumed there. It appears that the people quickly left the village after the killing.[12]

There is evidence of corpse mutilation in many other Anasazi sites, but deciphering if such horrible practices included cannibalism is difficult to discern. It could also have been the work of attacking tribes rather than the Anasazi themselves. Either way, the desecrated corpses testify to a dark and wicked practice that is frightening to consider.

The Cliff Palace in Colorado; it is the largest cliff dwelling site in North America

MYSTERIOUS ABANDONMENT

By the year A.D. 1300, the Anasazi were no more. The amazing cliff dwellings were abandoned and great trade centers were emptied of their wares and citizens. Researchers still don't know why the people moved on. Some theorize that a great drought forced them to leave, others see indications of a bizarre religious movement that drew thousands south. Maybe the people were fleeing the horrifying cannibalism or other evil practices.

Whatever the reason, the people dispersed and eventually the modern-day Pueblo people formed out of their descendants. Nobody ever moved back into the abandoned dwellings, and today they rest in haunted silence, void of life but full of mystery.

Incredible views from the cliff structures

Aztec

[A.D. 1100–1500]

The Aztec civilization was a powerful empire similar in characteristics to the early Akkadian Empire of Sargon (page 26). The Aztec civilization was made up of many different people groups, but one group, the Mexica, ruled the empire of city-states from their great city of Tenochtitlan (to become Mexico City in modern times).[13]

The Mexica people arrived in Mesoamerica from the north around A.D. 1110 but didn't settle in Tenochtitlan until around A.D. 1300. Eventually, the people of Tenochtitlan formed a "Triple Alliance" with two of their neighboring cities, but Tenochtitlan was the military power of the region. They went about conquering the other cities and regions of Mexico, eventually ruling almost 500 city-states and extending into other areas of Central America. It is likely that the Aztecs would have continued to flourish and grow, had the Spanish never arrived bringing war and disease that eventually vanquished their empire in A.D. 1521.[14]

The Role of Religion

The Aztec civilization was heavily influenced by their religious beliefs. Their religion was all about maintaining the balance between creation, the gods, and man. They had a great dread of nature and an irrational fear of the end of the world.

The Aztec believed that the gods had sacrificed themselves in order to create the sun and to allow humans to live on the earth. But they also believed that mankind was now responsible to repay this sacrifice by keeping the sun moving. They were required to sacrifice blood through either blood-letting or human sacrifice.[15]

13 "The Aztec Empire," http://www.aztec-history.com/aztec-empire.html, accessed October 9, 2014.
14 "Aztec Timeline," http://www.aztec-history.com/aztec-timeline.html, accessed October 9, 2014.
15 "Ancient Aztec Religion," http://www.aztec-history.com/ancient-aztec-religion.html, accessed October 9, 2014.

Ik Kil Cenote Well of Sacrifice

For the Aztec, there existed a constant battle in the sky between light and darkness. Their warrior sun god was called Huitzilpochtli, and he needed blood sacrifice in order to win the battle against the darkness. When humans were sacrificed, they would rise and join him in this battle — this belief would lead to a drastic increase in human sacrifice over the years.

Because of the importance of these sacrifices, they became an essential part of Aztec life and culture. Warriors were held in high esteem because it was their main purpose to capture prisoners for sacrifice. It wasn't until a fighter captured his first prisoner that he was considered a real Aztec warrior. Capturing more prisoners led to greater status and rewards such as rank promotion and land ownership.

The Height of the Empire

Under the leader Tlacaelel, the Aztec empire rose to its great height in the 1400s. Tlacaelel literally rewrote history; he burned old history books and in his new version he emphasized that his people were chosen by the gods to provide their nourishment. Their patron god, Huitzilpochtli, was a god of war and it was their responsibility to help him win. This gave the people a sense of purpose (similar to the Assyrians); they were constantly at war in order to capture more prisoners for sacrifice. Tlacaelel even instigated the "Flower War," which involved ritual battles with other cities for the sole purpose of capturing prisoners.[16]

Life in the Aztec culture was one of order, but mostly through fear. Their world seemed constantly on the edge of chaos as they tried to avoid upsetting the balance of nature, and appeasing the gods.

It seems hard to believe that this barbaric culture, practicing such horrific human sacrifice on such a large scale, could also possess cultural refinements and educational practices that were unlike most other ancient civilizations. In the Aztec society, even though there were definite social classes, education was compulsory for all boys and girls. Everyone in the society was generally well-educated, and the people even had some choice in their pursuit of career. Though the roles of priests, teachers, doctors, and leaders were generally only available for nobility, the common people ranged from efficient farmers to successful merchants, artisans, athletes, and of course, honored warriors. Slaves could even work to purchase their own freedom and every child was born free.

The Aztecs had a rich culture in music, drama, poetry, art, and athletics, yet life was constantly overwhelmed with religious observances. The cycles of their calendar and the rituals associated with it were carefully observed by all. Living in the shadow of the great pyramids, where hundreds if not thousands of their fellow human beings were being sacrificed, must have had an effect on daily life as well.

Much of what is known about Aztec culture comes from codices, or books, from the colonial era following the Spanish conquest of the area. This scene from the *Tovar Codex* is one example of such a book. Much of these books are visual depictions, such as this scene representing an attack on four ancestral Aztec tribes by three armies of the Tepanec, the Chalco, and Xochimilca. The Aztecs did have written books, but these were destroyed or disintegrated over time.

16 "Aztec Flower War," http://www.aztec-history.com/aztec-flower-war.html, accessed October 9, 2014.

Skull sculpture in Templo Mayor, Mexico City

"God Houses"

Aztec temples were called *Teocalli*, meaning "God Houses." They were built as centers of worship where the people came to pray and sacrifice. Usually, large areas of the city would be separated and used for religious purposes with many different sacred buildings. The most famous of these structures are the large flat-topped pyramids with shrines built on top. It was at these shrines that human sacrifice was performed.

Aztec pyramids were intentionally designed with very steep sides so that one could not see the top of the pyramid unless it was climbed. This was to symbolize that the gods were far above mankind and the only way to get close to them was to ascend a pyramid.

The most important pyramid for the Aztec civilization was the Templo Mayor, the "Great Temple" in Tenochtitlan. It was built symbolically as a recreation of the "Hill of the Serpent" and had two large snakeheads guarding its central staircase.

Templo Mayor was built to honor Huitzilopochtli and Tlaloc (god of rain and fertility), and both these gods required frequent sacrifice. During its final renovation in the late 1400s, thousands of people were sacrificed (Aztec legend documents 84,000, but historians believe it was closer to 3,000).[17]

Some believe that it was this appalling practice of human sacrifice that contributed to the fall of the Aztec. First, by killing such large quantities of people, they greatly reduced their population — and especially their warriors. The brutal practice also caused fear and hatred from both their enemies and citizens, who were taken captive and sacrificed. When given the opportunity to join the Spanish, enemies like the powerful city-state of Tlaxcala were eager to fight against their Aztec neighbors. Finally, the Spanish were horrified by the practice and considered the Aztec an evil culture that deserved complete destruction.

17 "Templo Mayor," http://www.sacred-destinations.com/mexico/mexico-city-templo-mayor, accessed October 9, 2014.

THE INCA

[A.D. 1150–1550]

The Inca Empire was one of the greatest in South America. They were at their peak (from 1150 to 1550) when the Spanish invaded and conquered them. Their civilization was located in modern-day Peru, with great cities built on both the low and high ground. These master builders are primarily known for their cyclopean masonry as well as incredible sites, like Machu Picchu, located high above the plains.

"Losing yourself" through drugs, alcohol, or meditation causes you to let go of your own identity and "open up," and potentially allow something else to gain control. When people seek to contact the spiritual world through things like meditation, soothsaying, satanic worship, witchcraft, and sorcery, they are inviting real forces to interact with them!

THE SPIRIT WORLD

The Inca were a polytheistic civilization, believing that there was a god of every aspect of the earth. From the sun and moon to wind, lightning, and rain, all the forces and pieces of nature were representative of some kind of deity. Their creator was known as Viracocha, the supreme being, and after him were the "second tier" sky gods. The greatest of the sky gods was Inti, from whom the Inca kings claimed to be descended. As we have seen in other civilizations, the Inca kings ruled by "divine right," and to go against them was to forfeit your afterlife.

Inca mummy, Peru City

The Inca were fascinated with divination (speaking with spirits and the "other world"). They would attempt this communication through hallucinogenic drugs, which caused them to go into a trance-like state. This gave them the ability to "connect" with the other world. While many people would simply write this off as mere superstition, it may have been more than that. Other religions (Buddhism, for instance) also attempt this kind of communication, achieving a trance-like state to become more spiritual.

HOW MUCH DID THE SPIRITS GET INVOLVED?

People like the Inca sought after this connection. Their religion was anti-God and they sought to communicate with demonic forces that they saw as gods. We cannot dismiss this practice as mere religious rituals that never amounted to anything, because rulers, powers, and forces of darkness DO exist and they are NOT to be treated flippantly (Ephesians 6:12).

There are ancient legends about how enormous blocks were moved at the sound of a whistle. Structures like the Great Pyramid, the temple at Baalbek, Sacsayhuaman, and others were built using stones so large we would have trouble lifting them today. Could there have been some other force at work?

What about at Babel? Could the leaders have had contact with the spiritual world? Was Babel where that idea started? We know that pagan world beliefs have their foundation at Babel, and upon the scattering of the people these ideas went with them. Could contact with the spiritual realm have been one of them?

The Inca Empire produced some of the most impressive architectural feats not only in South

Machu Picchu shows remarkable sophistication in its design and architecture.

America, but in the entire world. Many of these structures have proven to be inexplicable enigmas and no one knows for sure how they were built! Could it be that Satan deceived them by "helping" them to build these incredible cities and held them entangled in his wicked, distorted kingdom?

MASTERS OF CYCLOPEAN MASONRY

The city of Cuzco, built at over 11,000 feet above sea level, was the capital of the Inca Empire and is famous for its use of "cyclopean" masonry. Cyclopean architecture is a style of construction that uses precisely cut stones fit together to create a structure without the use of mortar. This term was first used for the walls and structures built by the Mycenaean civilization in Greece (1400–1200 B.C.). The method creates very strong structures because it eliminates mortar, which is typically weaker than the stone it holds together.[18]

Machu Picchu and Sacsayhuaman were also built with impressive examples of cyclopean architecture. Both of these sites were built at high elevations; Machu Picchu was built at a location over 7,000 feet above sea level, and Sacsayhuaman is at 12,000 feet.[19]

MACHU PICCHU

Machu Picchu is located high up in the Andes Mountains and is in pristine condition because it is quite difficult to reach. Besides its Cyclopean architecture, this elevated city also contains elements of archaeoastronomy; this includes the entrance to a cave that only admits light before and after the winter solstice, coinciding with the ritual Capac Churi (the initiation of royal boys into manhood).[20]

18 "Cyclopean Masonry," http://www.britannica.com/EBchecked/topic/148097/cyclopean-masonry, accessed October 30, 2013.

19 "World Mysteries — Mystic Places: Sacsayhuaman, Cusco, Coricancha, Muyuqmarka," http://www.world-mysteries.com/mpl_9.htm, accessed October 29, 2013.
20 David S.P. Dearborn, Katharina J. Schreiber, and Raymond E. White, *American Antiquity*, Society for American Archaeology, 1987, http://www.jstor.org/discover/10.2307/281786?uid=2&uid=4&sid=21102852457993, accessed October 29, 2013.

The famous sundial at Machu Picchu, Peru; and the large number of different structures.

Sacsayhuaman

Sacsayhuaman is a large fortress-like structure that may be the most impressive example of cyclopean architecture ever discovered. Just over a mile away from Cuzco, it is believed to be a fortress, though some claim it was only constructed to complete the puma figure which can be seen from the air. The walls are absolutely massive and stunning to behold. They are flawlessly cut and fit together so perfectly that not even a blade of grass can fit between them.[21]

The stones used in the structure are extremely large as well, some weighing over 150 tons! The largest is 29 feet high and is thought to weigh 360 tons! The quarry from which these stones were cut is about ten miles away.[22] How the Inca cut these stones, moved them into place, and fit them together so perfectly is a mystery. When the conquistadors from Spain saw these ruins, even they were mystified as to how the supposedly "primitive" Inca could have built such structures.

When the Spaniards arrived, around A.D. 1530, they destroyed the Inca people. They stole their gold, executed their leaders, and tore down their buildings. They exploited the people and enslaved many. The spread of European diseases also decimated the population, and by the end of the 15th century, historians estimate a decline of approximately 90 percent from the pre-contact population.[23] It was a horrible and tragic end to a mighty people, yet reminiscent of all civilizations that live in rebellion to the one true God.

21 "World Mysteries — Mystic Places: Sacsayhuaman, Cusco, Coricancha, Muyuqmarka."
22 Tracking Ancient Man, "Sacsayhuaman Walls," http://www.ancient-hebrew.org/ancientman/1044.html, accessed October 29, 2013.
23 "Spanish Conquest of the Inca Empire," http://en.wikipedia.org/w/index.php?title=Spanish_conquest_of_the_Inca_Empire&oldid=630495063, accessed October 21, 2014.

The massive stones that make up the three tiers of the Sacsayhuaman fortress are unique in both their size and construction. There is no mortar holding the rocks together or filling any voids because the stones were cut to fit together perfectly. The rocks were possibly dragged by massive ropes to the site, and possibly by other means as well.

Panoramic image of the stones at Sacsayhuaman with Cusco in the background

chapter 10

INHABITING THE ISLANDS

As mentioned in chapter six, ancient man was traveling the oceans of the world far earlier than many historians would expect. The civilizations that arose on several distant islands testify to the skill and intelligence of ancient man and also portray the recognizable characteristics of Babel that these seafaring peoples brought with them across the waters.

POLYNESIANS

[A.D. 1000–1700]

It is now almost universally believed that the Polynesians populated the Pacific islands in Southeast Asia and explored to the coasts of the Americas. They are widely regarded as the most successful navigators and seafarers in history. Their primary vessel was known as the Te Puke. It was up to 60 feet long and was built with double hulls, providing increased stability even in the open seas.

As they spread out from the Asian coast, they settled every island in the Pacific (over a thousand islands) by A.D. 1280. Everywhere from Easter Island to Cook Islands, the Polynesians proved themselves to be very capable engineers.

Some researchers believe that the Polynesians even reached South America. Chicken bones in Chile were presumed to be earlier than the Spanish introduction of chickens to the Americas. Polynesians would take chickens with them on their long voyages as a main source of food. Sweet potatoes from Chile have also been found on Polynesian islands; they were not native to any of the islands they grew on. The Polynesians' unique boat construction was also used by the early natives of both California and Chile, further evidence of communication with the Americas.

ANCIENT JAVA

[A.D. 300–1600]

Along the equator in Southeast Asia is a vast archipelago of over 17,000 islands known today as the country of Indonesia. With the world's fourth-largest population, Indonesia is home to hundreds of people groups that have their roots in a variety of ancient cultures.[1] The island of Java holds many antiquities that give us insight into the past of one such ancient culture.

Although not as ancient as the Middle Eastern or European civilizations, the remains of archaic artifacts and structures on the island of Java suggest that some of the people who were dispersed at Babel made their way to the Indonesian islands quite early on.

In fact, it is possible that some used their ships to reach Java as early as 2000 B.C.! From all indication, they would have made their way from India and China, perhaps in more than one migration.

We know that when Hinduism and Buddhism were introduced to the island around A.D. 100, there

---

1   "Indonesia Facts," *National Geographic*, http://travel.nationalgeographic.com/travel/countries/indonesia-facts/.

was already an existing culture, and ancient Indian Sanskrit inscriptions on rocks found throughout Java suggest that there were flourishing kingdoms on the island by A.D. 300.

An Island of Temples

One of the most iconic characteristics of Java is the deeply religious nature of its inhabitants. When Hinduism and Buddhism were introduced to the natives, they seemed to adopt and meld them with their already-existing pagan beliefs. The plethora of ancient temples testify to the diversity of their religious devotion.

Candis (Indonesian term for temples, pronounced "Ch-ahn-dee") have been built for centuries on Java, the most prominent ones being constructed between the seventh and tenth century A.D. There are hundreds of monuments throughout Java that the people built to honor their various gods, spirits, kings, ancestors, and animals.

Indonesian people were also distinctly awed by mountains. Shrines and graves of ancient kings and even village rulers dating back to the 15th century A.D. have been found on the tops of high peaks.

The locals on the island of Java consider Mount Lawu to be the holiest mountain in the world. People travel far distances to climb its 10,000-foot-high summit to fast and pray to their ancestors' spirits. There are at least ten ancient complexes of stone terraces and walls on Lawu's top. The largest terrace is about 330 feet long and 65 feet wide. These structures were built around the time of Christ.[2]

As the different dynasties and kingdoms rose and fell through the centuries, each left their mark through their temple building. One of the great civilizations to grow in power and really prosper was the Mataram Kingdom (A.D. 700–900).[3] It was during this time that the great temple of Borobudur and the nearby complex of Prambanan were built.

Candi Sari (also known as Candi Bendah) buddhist temple in Prambanan valley on Java, Indonesia; built around A.D. 778

Sukuh temple, Java, Indonesia

Prambanan Temple at sunset, Central Java, Indonesia

2   Eric Oey, *Java: Garden of the East* (Hong Kong: Periplus Editions, 1995).
3   "Java Indonesia History: Prehistory and Early Kingdoms" http://www.javaindonesia.org/ general/java-indonesia-history-prehistory-early-kingdoms/, accessed October 7, 2014.

BOROBUDUR

The largest Buddhist building in the world, Borobudur, is also known as "the world mountain."[4] Built by the Sailendra dynasty (a Buddhist regime of the Mataram kingdom)[5] around A.D. 800, its massive symmetrical, multi-tiered structure, as well as its ornate reliefs and statues, testify to the intelligence of the ancient people who built it. Its structure is similar to that of a step pyramid, and it was built around the same time that the Mayan pyramids were being erected.

The building is said to represent the levels of "enlightenment"; each tier symbolizes the next step to reaching the state of "formlessness."[6] There are three main tiers representing the three superimposing spheres of the universe, according to Buddhist cosmology.

The first level, the pyramidal base, represents the "sphere of desires" where mankind is bound to his worldly desires and pleasures.

The second level contains five concentric square terraces, representing the "sphere of forms," in which man has learned to let go of desires but is still bound to name and form.

The third level is the "sphere of formlessness," symbolizing freedom from the physical world and its desires and illusions.[7] It is represented by the highest three circular platforms of the temple as well as the big stupa (a dome-shaped structure).

The structure uniquely blends the key concepts of Buddhism and Nirvana with the tiered buildings of ancient ancestor worship.

4 "Temple," *Art Asia*, http://artasia.www2.50megs.com/Indonesia/temple.htm, July 15, 2013.
5 "Sailendra," New World Encyclopedia, http://www.newworldencyclopedia.org/entry/Sailendra, November 1, 2014.
6 "Borobudur, Prambanan & Ratu Boko," http://www.borobudurpark.com/temple/borobudurTemple, accessed July 14, 2013..
7 "Borobudur . . . Guide to Enlightenment," http://www.pbs.org/treasuresoftheworld/borobudur/blevel_1/b3_enlightenment.html, accessed November 3, 2014.

Prambanan

Near Borobudur, Prambanan was also constructed around the same time by the Sanjaya dynasty of the Mataram kingdom. It is the largest temple complex in Java dedicated to the Hindu religion. Prambanan contains 224 incredibly designed and intricately decorated temples, with most of the monuments housing some kind of deity. The three most magnificent temples in the middle of the complex are dedicated to the Hindu trinity: Brahma, Shiva, and Vishnu.[8]

Similar to Borobudur, the complex has multiple concentric squares of small monuments surrounding the three large structures in the center. Each of these central temples was skillfully designed to look higher than they actually are.[9]

Though the structures of Prambanan and Borobudur are the most spectacular of Java's ancient monuments, the building of temples did not stop there. Between the eight and tenth centuries A.D. the Mataram kingdom erected many small temples throughout Java. After the Mataram kingdom fell, the Javanese people continued to build places of worship on the island.

From above Borobudur

Candi Sukuh

Though it was built much later, in the 15th century, the curious temple of Candi Sukuh bears a remarkable resemblance to several Mayan monuments in Mexico. Unlike most Javanese temples, it is a stone ziggurat that seems to represent a mountain. From all indications, it was a place of fertility worship (several of the carved images are explicitly sexual) not much different from the ancient temples of the Greeks and Central and South Americans.[10] The drastic difference in building style and sculptures remains a mystery and could mark a reappearance of the pre-Hindu animism that existed on the island 1,500 years earlier.

Javanese history is a confusing mix of integrated religions. In ancient times, the people mixed animism, ancestor worship, and worship of rocks and trees with Hindu and Buddhist influences. Although these belief systems are contradictory, they are sourced in the same counterfeit kingdom. Syncretism, the combining of multiple contradictory beliefs, has been part of Indonesian culture for centuries. They continually tried to honor multiple authorities that were in opposition to each other. Perhaps that is why there are so many temples and large temple complexes in Java. The people were trying to harmonize their contradictory beliefs and make everything work together and fit. Because they rejected the true God, they were left with anything and everything else.

8   "Prambanan Temple Compounds," http://whc.unesco.org/en/list/642, July 15, 2013.
9   Ibid.
10   Oey, *Java: Garden of the East.*

Easter Islands' incredible moai sculptures are still a source of mystery.

EASTER ISLAND
[A.D. 700–1600]

Located thousands of miles from the nearest coastline, Easter Island covers roughly 64 square miles in the middle of the South Pacific Ocean. Known as Rapa Nui to its earliest inhabitants, the small island has an intriguing history that ended in disaster.

Researchers believe that humans first arrived on Easter Island around A.D. 300–400. Back then, the island was apparently covered in a dense palm forest, completely unlike the somewhat desolate landscape that exists there today. It is likely that the first settlers started with a small population, but they eventually grew to be quite numerous, with population estimates ranging from 4,000 to 20,000. Research suggests that the islanders cultivated the land successfully and supported several classes of people: laborers, warriors, and priests.

From A.D. 700 to 1600, the people of Rapa Nui had succeeded in developing the civilization that was responsible for constructing the incredible "moai" that are scattered around the island. These enormous stone statues have made Easter Island famous and are the clearest evidence of an intelligent and thriving culture.[11]

STATUES OF MYSTERY

The moai have long been the subject of mystery and debate. They present a technological achievement that has been the cause of wonder among modern historians.

Almost 900 statues have been found on the island, but experts estimate that there are at least 1,000.[12] Though they average 13 feet in height, the largest

11 Bloch, Hannah. "Easter Island." - Pictures, More From National Geographic Magazine. July 1, 2012. Accessed May 11, 2015. http://ngm.nationalgeographic.com/2012/07/easter-island/bloch-text?source=news_easter_island_story.
12 "Did Easter Island Statues Walk? Or Rock and Roll?" Fox News, http://www.foxnews.com/scitech/2012/06/21/did-easter-island-statues-walk-or-rock-and-roll/, accessed January 28–February 12, 2013.

moai is 33 feet tall and weighs 74 tons! The statues were carved in a quarry and then transported around the island, apparently without wheels or animal labor.[13] Both the number and size of these moai clearly show that incredible engineers masterfully crafted them and yet their purpose is still unknown.

Interestingly, the moai all face inland. Many are placed near the island's coast, and yet none of the moai face the sea.[14] They also are not found on the two corners of the island, and are primarily located on flatter surfaces. Many moai have been discovered in transit from the quarry of Rano Raraku, and there are even some inside that are unfinished.[15]

There is evidence to suggest that the inhabitants destroyed the earliest statues as the builders created larger ones later on. Some have theorized that the moai were carved by each of the families of the island to watch over their villages. They may have become a sign of power and influence and caused competition among the inhabitants. Some of the later statues are thought to represent important figures who were deified after their deaths.[16]

By the late 1600s, the civilization on Rapa Nui was falling apart. Civil war and destruction marked this time period even before the first Europeans landed on the island. The creation of the moai stopped and many were toppled over or destroyed.

The population of the island was drastically reduced for unknown reasons. Some theorize that over-exploitation of the island resources led to their downfall. Perhaps the growing competition between rival chieftains to build the most impressive moai contributed — it would have required a great deal of wood (to transport the statues) and food (to feed the workers). Once the resources of the island were depleted, some suggest that civil war broke out.[17]

Another theory suggests that the island's forests were destroyed due to an infestation of Polynesian rats that arrived with the settlers. These rats had no predators other than the humans and thus experienced uninhibited population growth. Archaeologists have found marred palm nuts with gnaw marks created by rats. The theory suggests that these rats ate the palm nuts, which prevented the slow-growing trees from repopulating. Thus, even without the inhabitants using the wood, the rats alone could have led to the forests' demise.[18]

Either way, by the time European explorers discovered the island, the population numbered only around 3,000. The fabulous moai were desecrated and no longer watched over their citizens but lay toppled on the ground. And conditions only continued to get worse for the inhabitants of the island after contact with the Europeans, leaving us only to wonder how such a place could ever have supported a prosperous civilization.

**Re-erected tuff moai at Ahu Tahai
with restored scoria pukao (the hat) and replica coral eyes**

13 Damien Gayle, "Did Easter Island's Statues 'Walk' into Place? Controversial Theory Suggests the Megaliths Were Moved Like Fridge, Mail Online, http://www.dailymail.co.uk/sciencetech/article-2222376/Did-Easter-Islands-statues-walk-place-Controversial-theory-suggests-megaliths-moved-position-fridge.html, accessed January 28–February 12, 2013.
14 David Batty, "Easter Island Statues 'Walked' into Position, Say Experts, http://www.guardian.co.uk/science/2012/oct/25/easter-island-statues-walked-into-position, accessed January 28, 2013.
15 Ewen Callaway, "Easter Island Statues Might Have Been 'Walked' Out of Quarry," www.scientificamerican.com.http://www.scientificamerican.com/article.cfm?id=easter-island-statues-might-have-been-walked-out-of-quarry, accessed January 28–February 12, 2013.
16 "Easter Island," http://www.history.com/topics/easter-island, accessed October 7, 2014.
17 Hannah Bloch, "Easter Island — If They Could Only Talk," http://ngm.nationalgeographic.com/2012/07/easter-island/bloch-text?source=news_easter_island_story, accessed January 28–February 12, 2013.

18 Ibid.

How Were the Moai Moved?

One of the biggest mysteries of Easter Island that has stumped researchers for years is how the inhabitants transported the enormous moai all over the island. There are two primary theories that attempt to answer this question: the wooden sledge theory and the "walking" theory.

The wooden sledge theory

The first theory is that the moai were placed horizontally on a wooden sledge, which was then rolled over log rails. It may be the most prominent because it gives an explanation for the large-scale deforestation that took place.

The "walking" theory

There is another theory that correlates with the ancient tales told by the local population. According to legend, mostly discredited as mere fairy tale, the statues actually "walked" to their positions.[19]

This theory suggests that the moai were moved by tying three ropes to the moai's head, one on each side and one on the back. The statue would then be leaned forward and each side would pull, shifting the statue from side to side, rocking it, and creating forward motion.[20] The key to this technique relies on the belly of the statue, which, according to the theory, was designed specifically for this purpose. The belly provided the weight and center of gravity for the statue to move forward when it was rocked.[21] If the "walking" theory is correct, it not only correlates with the ancient legends, it also exhibits the ingenuity of ancient man.

19 Ibid.
20 Rossella Lorenzi, "Easter Island Statues Could Have 'Walked,' " http://news.discovery.com/history/archaeology/easter-island-statues-walked-121025.htm, accessed January 28, 2013.
21 Callaway, "Easter Island Statues Might Have Been 'Walke'" Out of Quarry."

Nan Madol
[A.D. 1200–1600]

To picture Nan Madol, imagine a city built on the ocean and rising up high over the surface of the water. The mysterious, abandoned series of structures built on top of a coral reef can be found near the small island of Pohnpei in Micronesia. Here there are stone walls, built up to 50 feet high in places, with no carvings, no paintings, and no ornate details at all. Only legends are left of the large civilization that once inhabited these structures.[22]

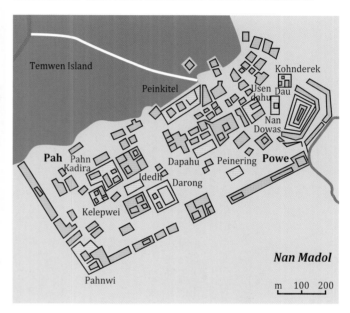

Nan Madol

"The Spaces Between"

Nan Madol means "the spaces between." The name refers to the canals zigzagging throughout and separating each artificial island structure.[23] The city is composed of 92 artificial islands spread over 200 acres abutting Pohnpei's mangrove-covered shore. Most of the structures were supposedly built between the 13th and 17th centuries by a population of less than 30,000 people. These ruins are clearly sophisticated in their engineering and design. They were built using naturally formed prismatic basalt columns and fitted together to form a strong, stacked wall.

22 Christopher Pala, "Nan Madol: The City Built on Coral Reefs," http://www.smithsonianmag.com/history-archaeology/Nan-Madol-The-City-Built-on-Coral-Reefs.html?c=y&page=2, accessed September 6, 2013.
23 Dr. Von Zuko, "The Lost City of Nan Madol," http://www.zuko.com/CrypticSphere/Lost_Civilizations_Nan_Madol.asp, accessed September 6, 2013.

Who Lived in Nan Madol?

The Saudeleur people supposedly inhabited Nan Madol for more than a millennium until they were finally wiped out in the 17th century. According to legend, it was built by two magical brothers who came to Pohnpei and wanted to create a unified political structure. Nan Madol was their capital city, from which they could rule their kingdom. They supposedly imposed their own religion on the people, and as time went on, their descendants became increasingly more tyrannical, eventually leading to unrest and rebellion.[24]

This culture adored and even worshiped the sea. They considered eels holy, and their priests would ritually feed them turtle innards at a sacred well located on one of their islands.[25]

24 "Nan Madol Ruins," Pohnpei Eco-Adventure, http://www.pohnpei-adventure.com/nan-madol/, accessed November 3, 2014.
25 Ibid.

122

COMPARABLE TO THE PYRAMIDS OF EGYPT?

Archaeologist and researcher Dr. Rufino Mauricio explains that the effort spent on these structures was greater than that needed for the construction of the pyramids of Egypt![26] The massive stones and columns used in the construction of the artificial landforms were probably moved from the other side of the island of Pohnpei. Researcher Christopher Pala explains that "the total weight of the black rocks moved is estimated at 750,000 metric tons, an average of 1,850 tons a year over four centuries."[27] These builders were not even credited with having pulleys, levers, or metal to aid them in their work.

HOW DID THEY MOVE THOSE STONES?

So far, researchers have no idea how the columns were brought to the site nor how they were lifted to build the walls. Most locals of the area believe the architects used magic to fly them into place, as the legend says.[28]

This solution is not unique to these people. Methods of magic, humming, drumming, or whistling have been described as ways to move stones in several cultures such as the Aymara Indians at Tiahuanaco, the creators of the Easter Island moai, the Inca, and even the builders of the Great Pyramid. These techniques have also supposedly been harnessed by Tibetan monks.[29]

Was this a demonic power? Was Satan using this to keep people distracted by their own accomplishment and pride so as not to turn to God and rely on Him? Nan Madol is yet another site of evidence backing up the idea that ancient cultures were more intelligent than we give them credit for. They were creative engineers, strategic builders, and skilled travelers.

An amazing example of the stonework at Nan Madol (and on the previous page)

26 Pala, "Nan Madol: The City Built on Coral Reefs."
27 Ibid.
28 Ibid.

29 David Pratt, "Gravity and Antigravity," http://davidpratt.info/gravity2.htm, accessed September 6, 2013.

chapter 11

"*Choose this day whom you will serve . . .*"

—*Joshua 24:15*

ONLY TWO KINGDOMS

You have now read a relatively brief history of man and hopefully you have been able to discern the underlying, man-centered philosophy that we have identified with the rebellion at Babel. The thread of man reaching for autonomy and rejecting God continues throughout the generations of Noah's children.

We have analyzed the cultures in history and pointed out where and how they rebelled against God. We have done this with a particular goal in mind: to open the eyes of the reader to see how history constantly repeats itself. If you recall the quote earlier in the preface of this book, Niccolo Machiavelli once said,

> Consult the past; for human events ever resemble those of preceding times. This arises from the fact that they are produced by men who ever have been, and ever shall be, animated by the same passions, and thus they necessarily have the same results.[1]

This quote lines up directly with a verse found in Ecclesiastes 1:9: "What has been is what will be, and what has been done is what will be done. . . ."

UNDERSTANDING OUR WORLD

In order to understand the world that we live in today we must first understand the past. In this book we have attempted to bring you back to one of the most critical points in human history: the rebellion at the Tower of Babel. Adam and Eve brought sin into the world, and those who existed before the Flood continued in that sin. After the Flood, however, something unique took place at Babel. Mankind came together and sought to replace God with themselves (though they were really replacing God with Satan — remember there are only two kingdoms).

At Babel, man took into account the person of God and directly sought to oppose and usurp Him. They did this by coming together (unity), building a city (a political agenda of a one-world, anti-god government), building a tower (a religious ideology centered on mankind usurping God), and making a name for themselves (humanistic philosophy directly opposing God). God ended their endeavor by confusing their languages. The people disbanded and traveled throughout the world forming different people groups with seemingly different ideologies. However, because they also carried their rebellious spirit toward God, we can see how the humanistic philosophy that began at Babel continued to show up countless times in ancient civilizations from around the globe:

Humanistic Philosophy	
The Minoans	naturalism
Assyrians	brutality
Rome	power and god-like status
Greece	humanism and relativism
Mede-Persia	tolerance
Israel	idolatry
Java	mixing opposing truths

Therefore, knowing how these themes of rebellion, such as relativism, tolerance, naturalism, and ultimately humanism, have shown up in ancient civilizations, we would like to challenge you to think about how each of these has affected the present day. Does the humanistic rebellion of Babel show up in our modern Western culture?

Let's take a look. These are just four examples of how anti-God philosophies are saturating our culture. Look at the civilizations listed in this book and how they turned their backs on God, and see if you can determine the different ways our Western culture today does the exact same thing as the ancient people. When you study history, look for the two kingdoms. When you watch movies, see if you can

1   "Learning from History," http://www.age-of-the-sage.org/philosophy/history/learning_from_history.html, accessed January 26, 2013.

identify what worldview and philosophy is being portrayed. Learn to analyze the world around you and see how it compares with the past. We hope that this book can give you a starting point and a basis for analyzing history and the present world.

Relativism ▶ Relativism is the idea that there is no such thing as absolute truth; "truth" is merely "relative" to each individual person. This is a very common belief in today's Western culture. Relativism attempts to relieve the tension between differing ideas, so people use it to defend any action they may take. Yet it breaks down, because we all know that truth is not relative; to say there is no absolute truth is an absolute truth statement. It proves the verse found in Romans 1:22 which says, "Claiming to be wise, they became fools."

Tolerance is closely connected to relativism. Today, tolerance may be among the most widespread positions in our culture. Unfortunately, the people who claim to be tolerant often find themselves on the opposite side of tolerance. Tolerance is the idea that even if people hold opposing views, they should still be "tolerant" and respectful of each other and therefore avoid any conflict.

Tolerance ▶ However, the secular world has pushed it even further and now tolerance means that all views are equal and equally true. This simply resorts back to relativism, in which truth is determined individually and therefore everyone can be "right." Accordingly, people are often intolerant of others who disagree with them and people who stand for such things as absolute, exclusive truth and morality. This intolerant tolerance provides more evidence that man knows God exists but is suppressing the truth in unrighteousness to serve his own purposes.

Naturalism is another view that has been prevalent throughout time and into the present, though it has come under many guises. In the past, people worshiped nature (Romans 1:22), literally bowing down to creation (such as the sun) — seeing the natural world as a god/gods. Today, people don't do that exactly, however they do worship nature in a different way, through evolution, extreme environmentalism, and materialism.

Naturalism ▶ Evolution is man's way of explaining how the world came to be without any divine intervention. Naturalists have extricated God from His creation. They view the world in a way that heightens the power of nature and materialist "cause and effect." It is essentially the same thing as what people in the past did when they bowed down to the sun. In the desire to suppress the existence of the transcendent God, people have replaced Him with creation. In the past, they did it directly through worship, now they do it by removing the supernatural and viewing everything in a naturalistic fashion.

Humanism is what most other "isms" eventually reach once you dig down into them. Humanism is the belief that man is the measure of all things. Therefore, mankind determines all truth, reality, philosophy, religion, etc. It is the removal of God as the ultimate authority and places man in God's place. It could be said that all sin is humanistic. Think back to the Garden of Eden when Adam and Eve accepted Satan's offer; Adam and Eve's disobedience came from the decision to follow their own desires instead of obeying God's command. They

Humanism ▶ placed themselves in the position of authority to determine what was right.

Today we fall into this same sinful humanism all too often. Day in and day out we are bombarded with this philosophy from movies and commercials to the very public education system that kids grow up in. Everything screams, "Do it your own way, make your own decisions . . . it's all about you!" God's way is in stark contrast to this humanistic thought process — we are to be obedient to Him, submitting and dying to self, recognizing Him as the ultimate authority and the measure of all things.

BUILDING A NAME

As we conclude this book we would like to summarize for you what God meant when He recorded for us that the people at Babel were coming together at the tower to build a name.

> They said, "Come, let us build for ourselves a city, and a tower whose top will reach into heaven, and let us make for ourselves a name, otherwise we will be scattered abroad over the face of the whole earth" (Genesis 11:4; NASB).

As discussed, Adam and Eve rejected God and fell for the suggestion that they could make their own decisions, do things their own way, and discover true knowledge — thus positioning themselves as being their own gods.

We believe that at the Tower of Babel, individuals with this heart of rebellion gathered together as an organized group and began a collective movement against God. The tower and the city refer to the physical accomplishments, and the "building of a name" refers to a general attitude and desire to build their own system of thought: a worldview based on the premise that they could be their own gods. Man's attempt to make for himself a name — whether individually or collectively — is an act of rebellion against, and a rejection of, God.

All through the Bible God makes a big issue of His name and names in general (as discussed in chapter 2 in more detail).

▷ Each of His names represents who He is and tells us of His nature, character, and attributes.

▷ We are not to take His name in vain (Exodus 20:7).

▷ We are to pray in the name of Jesus — in line with who and what He is (John 14:13–14).

▷ There is only one Name under heaven by which we might be saved (Acts 4:12).

▷ When we get to heaven we will find that even Jesus has a name that no one knows (Revelation 19:12).

▷ All believers will receive a new name as well (Revelation 2:17; Isaiah 62:2).

An illustration by Matthias Gerung showing the Fall of Babylon from Revelations in the Ottheinrich Bible, a beautiful illuminated manuscript from the 15th –16th Centuries in Bavaria.

In contrast, at the Tower, man made a statement of opposition to all that God is when they decided to "build for themselves a name."

In this book we have endeavored to show that throughout human history men, with this same rebellion in their hearts, gather together to form cultures that carry similarities to Babel. Time and time again we see man attempting to make a name for himself, placing humanity on a pedestal and raising man up to godlike status.

Each of us are born with a heart of rebellion against God, and many times in human history we can see this popularized in civilizations. At Babel and many nations down through history we see men rejecting God and attempting to discover knowledge, truth, and purpose on their own — to be their own gods. For whole nations, or individuals, the results are the same (page 25).

Thus history becomes a warning to all of us of the importance to "choose this day whom you will serve" (Joshua 24:15).

The Bible is clear; there is exclusivity about our God. There is, after all, only one God. And so we see His way, His purpose, and His truth as presented to us as all in accord with His Name. His Name represents Him.

Are you trying to build your own name? Are you setting up your own philosophy or way of thinking? Are you trusting in your own ability or system? It is a dead end. It was for Adam and Eve and for the people at Babel, and for every humanistic thought or practice since. It is true for us as well. Will you heed the warning we have been given through the record of history?

> There is a way which seems right to a man, but its end is the way of death (Proverbs 14:12, 16:25).

All the Treasures of Wisdom and Knowledge

Is there hope in the midst of all this sin and rebellion? The genius of ancient man with all his secrets and seductive influence is pointing us somewhere. Satan has been actively working for thousands of years to bring his kingdom to full power, but we know that ultimately Christ will reign over all and His kingdom will prevail.

Historically, man has sought to build a life and future without God, and it ends in tragedy. Cities and nations and civilizations have searched desperately for a way to meet man's inner needs and bring him hope, truth, and life. But a world system built upon fallible beings cannot find answers that bring fulfillment. A world that has set itself on a path of pursuing its own desires has led us through centuries of power-hungry dictators, human enslavement, persecution, empty philosophy, war, false and deceptive worship, poverty, and is ultimately nowhere nearer to happiness, purpose, and meaning. All of the efforts of man-centered progress have proven the inability to meet man's need or bring him everlasting hope.

The amazing fact is, our desire for truth and our desperate search to understand the secrets and mysteries of life on our own, can be answered in Christ! Whereas Satan constantly tempts with the unknown, offering secret knowledge but never fulfilling his promise and only leading us only deeper into darkness, God offers the answers in a fulfilling, transparent way that is clear and open to all.

Paul, in Colossians, states that the true knowledge of God's mystery is CHRIST "in whom are hidden all the treasures of wisdom and knowledge" (2:3). He warns the Colossians not to be taken captive "through philosophy and empty deception, according to the tradition of men, according to the elementary principles of the world" (2:8; NASB).

This message to the church in Colossae could have been preached to mankind in every century of human history! We seem so eager to be taken captive by empty, deceptive ideas like relativism, humanism, and evolution.

Times haven't changed. Satan has ensnared mankind, deluding ancient man and those of us in modern times through his deceptive philosophy and empty counterfeit. We have looked to ourselves rather than Christ; we raise ourselves up as the authority when, in fact, He is the head. The world needs Him!

Yet we are helpless to change any of this solely on our own. God is the One who calls and brings people to Himself. The Word of God and the Holy Spirit do the work of conviction, and faith allows us to believe. Though times may seem hopeless and worse now than ever before, man has been in this state since the Fall of Adam and Eve. There is still that gulf between guilty sinner and sinless Savior. There is still only one bridge: Christ, who died for us. And we, as Christians, are called to give a defense, to be ready, and to share the gospel. We cannot save anyone on our own, but we can shine and defend and love and speak.

Christ alone is the hope.

> But sanctify Christ as the Lord in your hearts, always being ready to make a defense to everyone who asks you to give an account for the hope that is in you, yet with gentleness and reverence (1 Peter 3:15; NASB).

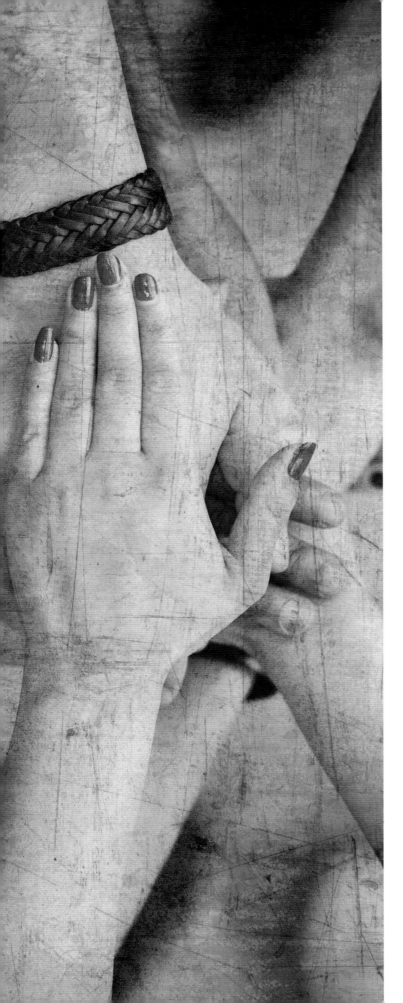

INDEX

Pastor Don Landis is the president of Jackson Hole Bible College and serves as pastor/teacher of Community Bible Church. He is also the founding chairman of the board of Answers in Genesis. He has been teaching on ancient man subjects for many years at JHBC. He and his wife Beverly live in Jackson Hole, Wyoming where they live with their two daughters, son-in-laws and families.

Analea Styles lives in Abbotsford, British Columbia where she works in the High School Youth Ministry at Northview Community Church. She grew up in Canada but after high school she attended Jackson Hole Bible College in Wyoming for their one-year Biblical Foundations program, graduating in 2011. She joined the Ancient Man Team as writer and editor of *The Genius of Ancient Man* and continues this work on the Ancient Man blog and ongoing projects. Analea earned a Certificate in New Media Journalism from Simon Fraser University and is excited to see God use her gifts to reach people and bring glory to His Name.

Matthew Zuk is a writer, editor, and researcher on the Ancient Man team. He is also currently serving as a teacher's aide at Jackson Hole Christian Academy. He grew up in upstate New York before moving to Russia as a missionary kid with his parents at eight years old. He moved back to America after nine years on the mission field and graduated from JHBC in 2013. His desire is to serve God and glorify Him in everything, keeping Christ and the Gospel as the focus (only by God's grace).

Derrick Zuk is the Communications Specialist (IT/AV/Social Media) at Jackson Hole Bible College and Community Bible Church. He also serves as an Assistant RA at JHBC and is the Missions Chairperson at CBC.

Derrick grew up in Upstate New York before moving to Russia with his family in 2003 when his parents became full-time missionaries. He attended Jackson Hole Bible College in 2010-2011 and graduated with a Biblical Foundations Diploma. He was a content editor for *The Genius of Ancient Man,* and currently serves as blog administrator and coordinator/editor for Ancient Man writing projects.

Timothy Thornton is the men's head RA at Jackson Hole Bible College where he earned his Biblical Foundations diploma in 2012. Tim grew up in the country of Indonesia as a missionary kid, and he has been living in the United States for three years. He desires to bring God glory with the use of his gifts and abilities as a researcher, author, and editor for the blog and other Ancient Man projects. Tim wants others to come to a saving faith in the Lord Jesus Christ and also to learn to love God and His authoritative Word.

Heidi Grosch earned her Biblical Foundations diploma in 2013 after coming to JHBC with a strong interest in geology and biblical studies. She then joined the Ancient Man team the following year to illustrate maps and charts for the project. Heidi has had a diverse background from topographic mapping to preparing artwork for college textbooks and always wondered how God could put the two backgrounds together. She desires to surrender her life to Him in everything.

Bethany Youngblood Ancient civilizations have captivated this Florida native since she was little and the desire to learn more has never gone away. She served as a part of the Ancient Man research team during her year at Jackson Hole Bible College. After she graduated in 2012, she continued to show interest in the project and looks forward to helping with research and posting to the blog. Her desire is to write historical fiction highlighting the intelligence of ancient man, and to give God the glory through her life and work.

Brian Mariani graduated from Illinois State University with a Bachelor's degree in Physics Teaching. He also graduated from Jackson Hole Bible College with a Diploma of Biblical Foundations in 2010. Brian then went on to teach high school science at a Christian school. He did research and writing for *The Genius of Ancient Man.*

Brian is now a Creation Evangelist working for Alpha Omega Institute teaching people about the evidences confirming the truth of the Bible. He, his wife Aimee, and their son Caden travel across the country teaching groups and churches about God's Creation, Ancient Man, the Challenges to Evolution, and more.

JACKSON HOLE, WY

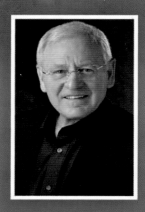

"JHBC's mission is to give a schematic overview of God's Word in a regular two-semester school year. We desire to teach our students a worldview that will provide a solid foundation for Biblical decision-making throughout every area of life. We wish for our students to be challenged in their academic pursuits but more importantly we desire their spiritual lives to be strengthened and challenged by constant exposure to the never-changing Word of God."

Don Landis
President of JHBC, General Editor of The Genius of Ancient Man,
Chairman of the Board of Answers in Genesis

"I am really thrilled to see a Bible college like Jackson Hole Bible College teaching young people to stand on the authority of the Word of God beginning right at the very first verse. They get practical training like you would never get at any other college I know of. It's a unique opportunity. They'll never forget it, it'll be with them for the rest of their lives."

Ken Ham
President & CEO of
Answers in Genesis

ONE FOUNDATIONAL YEAR OF BIBLICAL STUDIES AND PRACTICAL CREATION APOLOGETICS

FIELD TRIPS INCLUDED:
- Mt. Saint Helens
- Yellowstone NP
- Arches NP
- Canyonlands NP
- Natural Bridges
- Grand Canyon NP
- Zion NP
- Bryce Canyon NP
And many more stops!

CREDITS TRANSFER TO:
- The Master's College
- Cairns University
- Emmaus Bible College
- Arizona Christian University
- Montana Bible College
Others possible on case by case basis

 www.jhbc.edu   facebook.com/JacksonHoleBibleCollege   (307) 739-8630   jhbc.admin@gmail.com

DISCOVER MORE ABOUT
The Genius of
ANCIENT MAN

Follow our blog!

geniusofancientman.blogspot.com

ALSO AVAILABLE
FROM DON LANDIS
WITH JACKSON HOLE BIBLE COLLEGE

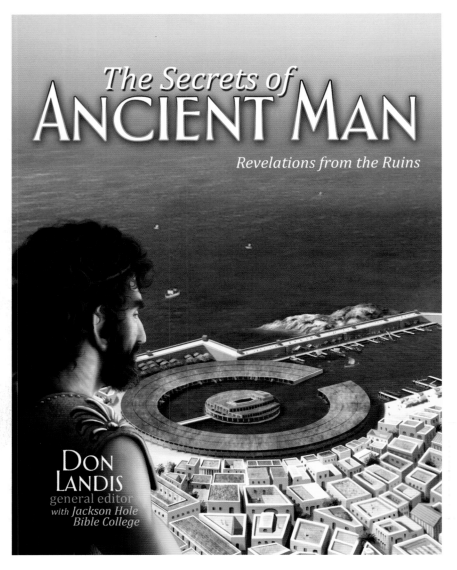

Full-color, Casebound **$21.99** | 978-0-89051-866-3

A "behind-the-scenes" look at the history of what ancient people did, as well as compelling questions and answers about why they did it!

"Gobekli Tepe is ancient ambiguity at its best! Mostly unknowns and fascinating questions, the people who constructed this site left a puzzling legacy in the semi-deserts of Turkey. For years, researchers tried to uncover the mysteries of this site and now what lies buried has been revealed: 20 megalithic stone-walled rings....When we operate under the biblical presupposition that man was created in the image of God, highly intelligent and creative, around 6,000 years ago, sites like Gobekli Tepe are not shocking to find."

—*The Secrets of Ancient Man*

Don Landis

President of Jackson Hole Bible College, Senior Pastor, & Answers in Genesis Chairman of the Board